YOUR MIND, YOUR UNIVERSE

A New Model of Consciousness That Unites Time, Reality, and the Soul

By

Brandon M. Procak

YOUR MIND, YOUR UNIVERSE

YOUR MIND, YOUR UNIVERSE

A New Model of Consciousness That Unites Time, Reality, and the Soul

By

Brandon M. Procak

Quaderer Media Group
175 Varick Street
New York, NY 10014

Your Mind, Your Universe

Published by Quaderer Media Group
175 Varick Street, New York NY 10014
www.quaderer.com

First Edition: July, 2025
ISBN: 979-8-9916659-4-0

Cover design by Claudine Mansour

Library of Congress Control Number: 2025940102

For information about special discounts for bulk purchases, please contact info@
quaderer.com.

Printed in the United States of America

INTRODUCTION

I used to think I had an epiphany—one of those aha moments you don't forget. I was sitting on my couch, reflecting on Einstein's theory of special relativity. It describes how time slows as an object accelerates toward the speed of light. But something struck me: We also experience time slowing under very different conditions—internally.

In moments of awe.
Looking into the eyes of someone you love.
In the middle of a crisis.
When you're fully immersed in what you love.

Time bends, not in space but in consciousness.

In that moment I didn't realize it, but I was glimpsing something deeper than physics.

Not time as a measurement but time as a mirror.

And not just bending through velocity, as Einstein showed, but through awareness.

What if your **state of consciousness** is the true variable in how time unfolds?

At the time I thought it was a new idea. But as I began writing this book, I dug up a journal entry from over twenty-five years ago. On the first page, I had scribbled a question.

What is the relationship between time, space, and consciousness?

That wasn't a passing curiosity. It was the seed. A question that would echo through decades of study, searching, and synthesis. A question that, unbeknownst to me, would become the core of everything that follows in this book.

This book is the product of twenty-five years of following that question across disciplines.

But this isn't a textbook. It's not trying to explain the universe from the outside.
It's trying to **reconnect you to it from the inside**.

You don't need a PhD to understand this.

You just need a pulse—and the willingness to wonder again.

This book draws from physics, neurology, philosophy, spirituality, and systems theory, but more than that, it attempts to reunite them. Because somewhere along the way, we split reality apart.

- Physics became divorced from consciousness.
- Psychology, from soul.
- Medicine, from energy.
- Philosophy, from resonance.

We now live in silos. Specialization has given us depth—but at the cost of wholeness.

But it wasn't always this way.

In ancient Egypt, the high priest was also the physician, the astronomer, and the mathematician.

In Greece, Pythagoras taught that numbers were sacred, geometry was the language of the divine, and music (especially the octave) was derived from both number and geometry.

In Vedic India, consciousness, breath, and cosmology were studied together.

In Taoist China, the sage was botanist, alchemist, healer, and poet.

The universe is not compartmentalized. It is continuous.

And so is this book.

We've tried to build skyscrapers on fractured ground—theories without soul, rituals without science, healing without wholeness.

This book is an attempt to weave it back together. Not to return to the past but to **restore the pattern**—the one that's been here all along.

This is where neurology meets nebulas.
Where spirituality meets frequency.
Where physics meets consciousness.
Where philosophy meets vibration.

Your Mind, Your Universe is both a theory and an invitation.

Chapters 1 through 5 lay the groundwork for what I call conscious resonance theory (CR)—a model that weaves together insights from quantum physics, brain science, cymatics, metaphysics, and ancient spiritual teachings. From chapter 6 onward, we shift from understanding to action.

CR suggests that reality is not something you just casually observe—it's something you shape and mold through your awareness. Minute by minute, breath by breath.

This is not a repackaging of the law of attraction, though you'll see how principles of manifestation naturally emerge within it. CR not only encompasses those ideas but also extends far beyond them. It doesn't just ask you to "visualize" or "believe."

It explains *why* your beliefs shape experience—mechanically, neurologically, vibrationally.

The law of attraction told us our thoughts create reality. CR shows *how*.

It brings precision to intuition. Structure to feeling. And a scientific framework to what mystics, healers, and seekers have long known: *that consciousness and the cosmos are not separate forces but harmonics of one and the same field.*

CR doesn't just empower the individual. **It's about integration. About seeing the hidden blueprint beneath everything.**

It's not about wishful thinking. It's about purposeful participation.

And from that realization, a new kind of personal responsibility— and personal power—emerges.

This book is meant to shatter paradigms.
To invite awe. To spark curiosity.
To challenge the idea that we've already figured everything out.

It's not just a book of ideas. It's a mirror.

One that reflects what you already suspect:
That you are not a bystander in this universe.
You are a composer. A conductor. A participant in the field.

If this book succeeds at one thing, I hope it reminds you:
Curiosity is not a phase of childhood.
It's the compass of consciousness.

And the direction that compass points . . .

depends on you.

1

THE ILLUSION OF TIME

People like us, who believe in physics, know that
the distinction between past, present and future
is only a stubbornly persistent illusion.
—ALBERT EINSTEIN

THE SHIP THAT OUTRAN TIME

Imagine a spaceship departing Saturn, its rings glinting like ancient vinyl grooves beneath the black silence of space. The vessel lifts off slowly, then accelerates, silently gaining speed until it reaches a staggering 99.9999% of the speed of light.

Inside, life is calm. The crew adjusts instruments, sips coffee, and chats about Earth politics they've left behind. They flip through photos of loved ones saved on their futuristic contact lenses. To them, it's just another return trip, a little over an hour maybe, before they'll be home again.

Seconds tick forward. Heartbeats stay steady. Thoughts pass as they always do.

But on Earth things are much different.

Outside that ship, reality is sprinting. The universe around them is in fast-forward. Empires are rising and falling. Technologies are born and forgotten. Languages go extinct. Weather patterns reshape coastlines. All in the span of that one quiet hour onboard—humanity forgets them.

When the ship lands, Earth has aged one thousand years.

Their homes are dust. The cities they knew are shadows. Humanity, if it exists at all, is unrecognizable.

They've stepped into the future.

This isn't fiction. It's not a screenplay or a dream. It's a natural consequence of motion.

Einstein taught us that time is not absolute. It is not the metronome of the universe, striking the same beat everywhere for everyone. It is elastic, flexible, strange.

The faster you move, the slower time flows for you. This is time dilation. It's as real as gravity, light, and heat. It is woven into the equations that govern the cosmos.

And perhaps more astonishing than the math is this:

Time is personal. It is as Einstein said: relative.

Two people in different conditions, moving at different speeds or experiencing different gravitational fields, live in different versions of "now." There is no single universal present time. There is only perspective.

Einstein's insight was this: Your experience of time is tied to your motion through space.

But what if it's tied to something even deeper?

What if your experience of time is also shaped by your state of awareness?

Since Einstein's work, we have always believed we need machines to break the bounds of time: faster rockets, stronger engines, warp drives, wormholes.

But what if the true vehicle isn't mechanical at all?

What if it is you?

EINSTEIN'S GIFT

In 1905 Albert Einstein offered humanity a new map of reality. His special theory of relativity revealed a truth stranger than any science fiction: Time is relative. The faster you move, the slower time passes for you compared with someone standing still.

This isn't speculation—it's measurable, observable, and already embedded in the technology that underpins modern life.

Take the International Space Station: Astronauts orbit Earth at over seventeen thousand miles per hour. According to Einstein's equations, that velocity slightly bends time in their favor. They age more slowly, by just fractions of a second, but measurably so. Over a six-month mission, an astronaut may age 0.005 seconds less than someone on Earth. It's minuscule, yes. But it's real.

Now scale that up.

Satellites powering GPS systems orbit at speeds and altitudes where both special and general relativity come into play. Left uncorrected, the clocks on these satellites would diverge from Earth's time by about 38 microseconds per day. That may sound negligible—until you realize GPS calculates your position based on precise time signals. Each microsecond error translates to a positional error of about one hundred feet. Without Einstein's corrections, your GPS app wouldn't just get you lost—it would place you miles away.

That's every Uber ride, every Amazon drone, every geotagged photograph. All of them rely on bending time to work correctly.

Before the equations, there was a thought.

As a teenager, Einstein imagined himself chasing a beam of light, riding alongside it, asking, "What would I see?" This seemingly childish curiosity unraveled the foundation of physics. Newton had imagined time as absolute: the same everywhere, for everyone, like a divine metronome ticking across the cosmos.

But Einstein's vision cracked that open.

He realized something odd: If you could somehow travel alongside a beam of light, moving just as fast as it does, the wave would appear frozen, stuck in place. But that made no sense. After all, light is supposed to move. So how could it ever look still?

This paradox led Einstein to a radical conclusion: No matter how fast you're moving, light always appears to travel at the same speed. That defies common sense—but it's true. And to make this consistent, something else had to adjust. That something was time. For light's speed to stay constant for all observers, time itself must slow down or speed up depending on your motion. The faster you go, the more time stretches.

This overturned over two hundred years of Newtonian certainty, effectively replacing his fixed, absolute laws of space and time with a new, dynamic understanding—all in one elegant stroke.

And it didn't stop there.

Einstein also discovered that **gravity affects time**. The stronger the gravitational pull around you, the slower time moves. That means a clock on Earth's surface, where gravity is stronger, actually ticks a little more slowly than a clock placed high up on a mountain. It's not that the clock is broken. It's that **time itself** is flowing differently in each place. The closer you are to a massive object (like a planet), the more gravity stretches time out.

And then there's the thought experiment that blew open popular awareness of this truth: the twin paradox.

Imagine two twins—identical in every way. One remains on Earth. The other boards a spacecraft and flies near the speed of light for several years, then returns.

To the traveler, only five years passed.

But for the twin who stayed on Earth, decades have passed. The traveler returns younger, perhaps by thirty years. Same DNA. Same twin. Different ages. Time bent more sharply for one than the other.

This isn't a trick of clocks—it's a trick of the universe itself.

Because here's the thing: Time is not a background feature of reality. It is not etched in stone. Time is shaped by motion and gravity, yes, but deeper still, it's shaped by perspective.

While standing on Earth, we all seem to experience time the same way—one second ticking into the next, twenty-four-hour days unfolding in steady rhythm. That's because we're all riding the same planetary vessel. Earth orbits the Sun, the Sun orbits the center of the Milky Way, and the Milky Way itself drifts through even larger superclusters. In total Earth is hurtling through space at roughly **1.3 million miles per hour**—and yet, because we share that motion, our experience of time feels synchronized. We set our calendars to seven-day weeks, organize life by hours and minutes, and call that "normal."

That's why Einstein's work was so revolutionary. He didn't just tweak equations—he broke the very metaphor we used to understand reality. Before him, time was imagined as a single, universal clock, ticking away identically for everyone, everywhere.

But Einstein showed us something stranger—and truer: There isn't one clock. There are many. Each person, each object, each location in the universe has its own timeline—its own rhythm—depending on how fast it's moving, how close it is to a gravitational field, and how it's being observed.

Your position in the cosmos—your velocity, altitude, and proximity to mass—literally changes the flow of time.

From that vantage, the world is no longer fixed in a single, synchronized "now." It becomes a tapestry of overlapping moments—woven together by perspective.

And that leads us to a deeper question.

If speed can stretch time,
And time bends according to perception,

Can consciousness?

THE MIND AS THE VESSEL

What if there's a way to alter the experience of time, not through motion and machinery but through something we're all acutely familiar with?

Consciousness itself.

We often think of time as a ruler laid across reality, something we move along with no choice but to follow. But if time can bend under the force of motion, as Einstein showed, then what role, if any, does perception play?

This is not just poetic language. Neurologically, time perception is intimately tied to consciousness. The brain doesn't possess a single "clock." Instead, it creates the illusion of time by tracking change, by measuring the intervals between stimuli, memories, and sensations. However, through meditation, trauma, awe, psychedelics, or hyperfocus, the brain constructs a different experience of time.

After all, haven't we all felt it?

Time races when we're in flow. A five-hour creative burst can vanish in what feels like five minutes. Or conversely, in moments of boredom, grief, or discomfort, minutes can stretch into eternities. Time slows, not because Earth moved differently but because we did—internally.

In those altered states, time can collapse or dilate.

Moments can stretch into something infinite.

Some call this flow. Some call it stillness.

We've all touched this, often when life is at its most intense or beautiful.

Ask a woman about the moment just before her child is born. Ask a musician mid-performance, lost in the swell of notes, unsure whether five minutes or an hour has passed. Ask someone who's been in a car crash—the instant before impact, when everything slows down and every detail becomes vivid, suspended.

Time doesn't feel measured in seconds then. It feels measured in presence.

Even our language gives it away: Time stood still, time flew by, time dragged on. These are not poetic flourishes—they're the brain's real-time reports.

Modern neuroscience supports this. Time perception isn't governed by a single clock in the brain. Instead, it emerges from a network of regions, each influenced by emotion, attention, and neurochemistry. When you're excited or fearful, levels of dopamine and norepinephrine spike. These neurotransmitters heighten alertness, sharpen focus, and expand sensory intake, flooding the brain with more data per moment. With more input to process, the brain stitches together a denser sequence of perceptual frames, making time feel stretched, as if it's moving in slow motion.[1, 2, 3]

Conversely, in low-stimulation or repetitive states, time contracts. The brain logs fewer data points, so hours vanish in a haze. It's not the hours that change—it's your conscious engagement with them.

So again, we ask:

What if the architecture of time is not only outside us but inside us too?

This opens a wild possibility.

If time is experienced through awareness, then it may be shaped by awareness.

And if it can be shaped, then it can be navigated.

In this light the mind is no longer just a passenger. It becomes the vessel. Like the spaceship in our earlier thought experiment, it can travel faster or slower depending on the terrain—except in this case, the terrain is your own state of being.

Let's entertain this further.

What if memory isn't just a container of the past but a vehicle for time travel?
And what if imagination isn't fantasy but a projector, letting awareness preview what hasn't yet happened?

What if the reason meditation feels timeless is because it is?

This book proposes something radical:

That consciousness is not merely a witness to time.
It is the lens that bends it.

Just as speed and gravity distort the external flow of time, the state of our awareness reshapes the internal experience of it.

Shift the lens, and you don't just see a new reality.

You *enter* one.

THE SEED OF A GREATER TRUTH

In Einstein's universe, motion through space bends time. The faster you move, the fewer frames of reality you experience. Events that once appeared continuous begin to separate, revealing the discrete, frame-like nature of time itself.

Physicists call this the relativity of simultaneity. What looks like "now" for you may be "later" or "earlier" for someone else, depending on how fast they're moving. Reality becomes a mosaic of frames—individual slices of space and time—stitched together differently depending on your path.

But this book invites us to consider something more intimate:

What if consciousness is the one doing the stitching?

Imagine a filmstrip. Each frame is a static image. Nothing moves. Nothing breathes. It is only when the film is projected at a certain speed that the illusion of motion—the illusion of continuity—emerges. Like a children's flip-book.

Reality may work the same way.

Each moment is a frame. Consciousness is the projector. Each moment is like a frame in a film—discrete, still, awaiting the motion of your awareness to bring it to life.

Your awareness moves from frame to frame, stitching them together into what you call your life. But it's not the frames alone that create the experience—it's the *quality* of the awareness playing those frames that shapes it.

Change the level of awareness, and the entire movie changes.

In deep meditation you may become aware of the frame itself—the silent seam between moments.

In trauma the stitching can lock, looping a single frame that haunts for a lifetime.

In near-death experiences the thread can leap forward, replaying an entire lifetime in an instant. And in moments of overwhelming joy or shock, the frames may vanish entirely, leaving only a blur—or a blank.

These aren't glitches. They're missing frames. Like déjà vu—the eerie sense that time has rewound, repeated, or momentarily disappeared—they aren't flaws in perception. They're clues. Clues that time isn't something happening *to* you.

It's something your mind assembles.

Because just as relativity showed us that the observer shapes time through motion, this book proposes that the observer shapes time through consciousness.

The quality of your consciousness is the dial that sets the frame rate—and that dial is tuned by your inner frequency.

So the question isn't just "What is time?"

It's also "Who is the one watching it unfold? What is their state of consciousness?"

This insight lies at the heart of this book: that time is not merely a property of the cosmos—it is also a cocreation between the physical world and the awareness that witnesses it.

Your consciousness is not passive. It does not simply witness. It weaves.

And what it weaves, moment by moment, is not just memory.
It's reality itself.

WHY CONSCIOUS RESONANCE THEORY IS NEEDED

Einstein gave us a framework to understand the external world. His equations explained how speed bends time, how gravity curves space, and how motion reshapes reality.

But his work—revolutionary as it was—stopped at the edge of the mind.

Physics, in its current form, does not yet account for awareness. It charts the motion of particles but says nothing of the presence observing them. It describes how time dilates in orbit but not how it feels and collapses in a moment of awe. It can model how clocks tick more slowly on a satellite but not why a single minute of heartbreak can feel like an hour or why joy evaporates time completely.

This is not a flaw in Einstein's genius. It is the incompleteness of our model.

Motion bends external time. But consciousness bends internal time.

And it always has.

Long before satellites, shamans and sages described altered time through ritual, trance, breathwork, fasting, and stillness. In every tradition—Vedic, Christian, Islamic, Taoist, Indigenous—there are accounts of time suspending, looping, or vanishing.

The language of physics is elegant, precise, and cold. But the language of experience is messy, ecstatic, and full of feeling.

Carl Jung wrote, "Who looks outside dreams; who looks inside awakes."

Teresa of Ávila, deep in mystical union, spoke of "the eternal moment" where hours disappear.

Aldous Huxley, under the influence of mescaline, described "eternity in a flower," time dissolving into a shimmering, seemingly endless now.

What science describes from the outside, these mystics describe from within.

We need both.

Conscious resonance theory (or CR) emerges not to replace Einstein but to extend him—to give language to subjective time, to build a bridge between neuron and nebula, between relativity and revelation.

Where classical relativity describes how mass and motion warp the fabric of space-time, CR proposes a parallel truth: that vibration of consciousness warps the frame rate of reality.

That your internal state—measured not in miles per hour but in resonance, awareness, and brain waves—can alter how time is perceived, felt, and even remembered.

When your awareness rises, your internal frequency increases—and with it, the quality of each frame you perceive. This is not symbolic. It's neurological. A gamma-state brain processes more data slices of *now*, creating a richer, slower, more detailed experience of time.

Just as an object in motion experiences fewer *external* frames of time, a being in heightened awareness slows *internal* time by perceiving more detail per moment. Both slow the progression of time—but one through speed, the other through presence.

The yogi in samadhi.
The artist in flow.
The child in play.
The lover in union.
The meditator in stillness.

Each of these experiences compresses, stretches, or dissolves time, not metaphorically but experientially. Because when consciousness is coherent, the projector runs differently. The resolution sharpens. Reality doesn't just feel different—it *is* different.

Without a framework such as CR, we are left with fragments—scientific insight on one side, mystical insight on the other.

But they are two halves of the same whole, and we've kept them apart for too long.

Today, knowledge is fractured. The physicist models space-time. The neurologist maps the brain. The psychologist tracks memory. The priest tends the soul. The physician treats the body. Each field has advanced in astonishing ways—but in isolation. Insights that belong together are studied in separate rooms, with separate languages and separate rules.

It wasn't always like this. In ancient cultures the priest was also the healer, the astronomer, the philosopher. One consciousness held the stars and the soul together. The body and cosmos were not divided— they were understood as reflections of one field.

CR doesn't just propose a new model of time. It proposes a return to wholeness.

14

CR reunites what we've broken apart. It offers a frame where particle physics and mysticism, neurology and memory, brain waves and destiny can all be part of the same sentence—not metaphorically but mechanically. It provides a common language between the inner and outer, between scientific pattern and spiritual presence.

It takes what we've dismissed as "woo" and makes it testable. What we've called objective, it makes personal. CR shows that our most intimate, subjective states are not anecdotal—they are measurable distortions in time, driven by resonance, focus, and coherence. CR is needed because without it, we remain scattered, each discipline solving a fragment while the human being remains a mystery.

Mystics have long described timelessness, altered states, and deep presence, but we now know these aren't just spiritual metaphors. Science has begun to catch up. Neuroscience confirms that perception of time shifts based on brain wave states. Psychologists measure how trauma warps memory and duration. Quantum physics reveals that observation changes outcome. Studies of flow states show measurable compression of perceived time.

In other words we can now measure what sages once only intuited.

We don't ask whether GPS satellites need Einstein's equations— they certainly do. Without those corrections, your location becomes meaningless.

In the same way, without a model such as CR, your place in time— your orientation to memory, meaning, and purpose—begins to unravel.

GPS needs Einstein.
Human clarity needs CR.

To make this distinction more concrete, here's a side-by-side comparison of Einstein's physical relativity and CR's awareness-based model:

EXHIBIT 1A

Einstein vs. Consciousness Relativity:
Time Dilation and Information Comparison

Aspect	Einsteinian Relativity	Consciousness Relativity (CR)
What bends time?	Physical speed / gravity	Vibration of consciousness
Where is the effect observed?	External (relative to observer)	Internal (subjective awareness)
Change in subject experience?	No (time feels normal to traveler)	Yes (richer, slower, deeper time)
Information per moment?	Constant	Increases with frequency
Perception of time?	Feels normal	Expands (more now-moments)
Mechanism?	Motion through spacetime	Frequency through mindspace
Information degradation?	No degradation (but no increase in clarity)	No degradation—clarity and coherence improve

Both models are true within their domains—one external, one internal. But together, they point to a deeper truth: **that time is warped not just by gravity and speed but by the mind that observes it.**

This is why CR is needed, not just to understand time but to reclaim authorship over it.

Without CR, we are excellent recorders of reality but poor authors. With CR, we remember we are both.

We are no longer merely watching the filmstrip of life.

We are realizing we hold the projector.

And what we project—through our frequency, focus, and feeling—becomes the life we live.

WHERE WE GO NEXT

By now something in you may already sense it:

Time isn't what we thought it was.

It is not fixed. It is not neutral. It is not an arrow moving in one direction.

Time bends with motion, yes. But it also bends with mind. It stretches with awareness, distorts with emotion, and dances with attention.

CR is not here to discard science—it is here to complete it.

It begins where physics ends: at the threshold of the observer.

In the chapters ahead, we will go deeper into this observer—this frequency—tuning awareness behind the projector, the one collapsing each frame into reality. We will explore how consciousness is not just a witness of the universe but a participant in its unfolding. We'll revisit the famous double-slit experiment, not just as a physics mystery but as a spiritual key.

We will study vibration, not as metaphor but as the architect of both matter and mind, mapping how it shapes sand, brain waves, emotion, and time itself.

We'll examine the architecture of the brain itself: its rhythms and waves, its quiet states and ecstatic ones, and how each corresponds to different experiences of time, memory, and even reality itself.

We will dive into altered states—what the mystics, the meditators, and even modern medicine have taught us about slipping out of clock-time into something vaster—where your awareness shifts the frame rate of reality itself.

We will study creation, not in the cosmic or religious sense alone but as a process that begins with awareness, for everything that has ever existed first appeared in consciousness.

And finally, we will touch the edge of something sacred: timelessness.

Werner Heisenberg once wrote, "What we observe is not nature itself, but nature exposed to our method of questioning."

What if time, space, and matter respond to how you see?
What if your very act of seeing changes what is seen?

Are you ready?

Let us begin.

RECAP: CHAPTER 1: THE ILLUSION OF TIME

Time is not absolute. Einstein showed us it bends with motion and gravity. But something deeper bends it too: **awareness**.

We've explored the following:

- Through Einstein, we learned that the faster you move, the fewer frames of time you experience.
- Your **consciousness**, like a projector, stitches reality together frame by frame.
- **Time is not a river flowing outside you—it's a rhythm shaped within you.**

- And just as motion alters external time, the **quality of your awareness alters internal time**.

This is the seed of **conscious resonance**—the idea that your state of being shapes your experience of time. With CR, we step beyond physics into perception, where every moment becomes a choice, a vibration, a creation.

In the next chapter, we'll begin to explore what this awareness truly is. Not just as an idea but as a force that collapses possibility into reality.

We'll meet the **observer**.

And everything will begin to change.

2

THE CONSCIOUS ARCHITECT

Not only is the universe stranger than we imagine—
it is stranger than we can imagine.
—Sir Arthur Eddington

THE QUANTUM RIDDLE AND LIGHT-WAVE COLLAPSE

The crew was nearly home from Saturn.

But what powered them wasn't rocket fuel or fusion.

It was the quantum sea itself.

They had learned to surf the quantum foam, where space-time trembles with uncertainty and particles flicker in and out of being like fireflies at the edge of thought. Their vessel didn't tear through space. It *folded through it*, guided not by engines but by consciousness.

At the core of their propulsion system was a chamber of suspended potential—quantum froth churned and tuned until space-time became pliable. The ship didn't push forward. It was pulled, drawn by probabilities collapsing in sequence, like stepping stones forming just ahead of each footfall.

As they approached Earth's atmosphere, one of the physicists aboard noticed it wasn't just time that had bent around them. It was matter itself.

Maybe they hadn't moved through space at all.

Maybe space had unraveled for them.

But how was this possible?

A STRANGER WORLD THAN WE EVER IMAGINED

For most of history, we believed the world to be solid, fixed, and predictable.

Rocks were rocks. Tables were tables. Objects behaved like, well, objects.

But the deeper science looked—down into atoms—the stranger things became.

Particles blink in and out of existence.

Matter turns out to be mostly empty space.

And just *observing* something changes what it is.

This isn't science fiction.

This is the world of modern quantum mechanics.

Quantum mechanics is the branch of physics that studies how reality behaves at the smallest scales—far smaller than atoms. At this level the rules are unlike anything we experience in everyday life. It's a science of the unseen, where outcomes aren't certain but *probable*.

Where light can be both a wave and a particle.

Where two things can be connected instantly across any distance.

And where consciousness might just play a role in what becomes real.

In short, quantum mechanics reveals a world that's not solid and mechanical but fluid, participatory, and deeply mysterious.

As we'll see in this chapter, experiments such as the double-slit test and quantum entanglement don't just hint at mystery—they *prove* it. They reveal that the universe is built not on certainty but on possibility. Not on hard edges but on waves of potential waiting to collapse into form.

It may feel like metaphor.

But it's real.

And once you begin to grasp what this means, it becomes clear: We are truly living in a strange world.

And more astonishing, we are *participants* in its unfolding.

To begin, let's return to something simple: a rock in your hand.

Let's look deeper and watch reality begin to dissolve.

THE ILLUSION OF SOLIDITY

Pick up a rock. It feels firm. Heavy. Real.

But zoom in, way in, and you'll find something shocking.

At the tiniest level, everything solid is mostly . . . empty.

Atoms make up all matter—rocks, tables, your body. But atoms aren't tiny balls packed together.

They're more like miniature solar systems. A dense center called the nucleus sits in the middle, and tiny electrons orbit far away.

How far?

If the nucleus were the size of a marble, the nearest electron would be almost a football field away. That's close to three hundred feet away from the marble!

That's like placing a grain of rice at the fifty-yard line in the middle of the stadium, and the next bit of "stuff" is dancing near the top row of the bleachers.

Everything in between?

Nothing. Just empty space.

In fact, atoms are more than 99.9999999999999% empty space.

So why doesn't your hand fall through a table, or why don't we fall through the floor?

Because of invisible forces—electromagnetic fields. When your hand gets close to an object, the atoms in your hand push against the atoms in the table, like magnets that repel each other. That push creates the *feeling* of touch.

But here's the twist: That feeling only shows up when you observe it.

It's not just that things *are* solid—it's that your consciousness creates the feeling of solidity.

Reality responds to attention. This is real science, not metaphor.[1] You're watching it *appear*—moment by moment, frame by frame.

How can this be?

To understand, we'll need to step into one of the strangest doors science has ever opened.

Not a portal through space but a doorway into the truth of reality itself.

THE DOUBLE-SLIT EXPERIMENT

Few experiments have shattered our understanding of reality like the now-famous double-slit experiment.

Let's begin with a metaphor.

Imagine a hallway with two doors: Door A and Door B.

A person, whom we'll call *Light*, walks toward them.

Naturally, you expect Light to choose one door or the other. But if *no one* is watching, something bizarre happens:

Light doesn't pick just one door.

Instead, Light seems to walk through *both* doors at once, like they've duplicated themselves.

And on the floor behind the doors, instead of two simple footprints, you see a strange, wavy pattern—like ripples where two stones landed in a pond.

It's as if Light took every possible path, all at once.

When unobserved, Light isn't choosing a single door. Light is entering Door A, Door B, both doors, even none. It's not making a single choice but expressing all possibilities through the form of a wave pattern. The wave is mapping every *possible* path.

Of course, this makes no sense in everyday life.

How could a person walk through all doors at once?

So now let's install a camera to see exactly what Light is doing.

And something even stranger happens.

The moment you watch to see which door Light chooses, everything changes.

Now they pick just one.

The wave pattern disappears, and we find two normal footprints that chose either Door A or Door B.

THE IMPLICATION?

Your attention matters—*literally*. Just by watching, you change what Light does. Before observation, Light exists as a wave—a spread of all possible outcomes. It could go left, right, both, or neither. Nothing is decided. Everything is potential. But the moment you look, that wave of possibilities collapses into one clear result: Door A. Or Door B. One path, one outcome.

In other words, the act of observation *creates reality.*
Your consciousness plays an active role.
It takes something uncertain and undefined—and forces it to choose.
A maybe becomes a yes.

It sounds impossible. But this is exactly what happens in real physics.

In the actual experiment, physicists fire tiny particles of light—called photons—at a barrier with two vertical slits.

If you don't measure or observe which slit the photon goes through, it behaves like a *wave*—spreading out, interfering with itself, and forming a ripple-like pattern on the screen behind.

It's as if the photon performs *all* possible outcomes at once.

But the moment you add a detector to measure which slit it chose, the ripple vanishes. The photon behaves like a *particle* again—choosing just one path and leaving a straightforward impact pattern.

And this collapse doesn't only apply to photons. It holds true for electrons, atoms, and even large molecules.

The strange truth is that the building blocks of our reality—these particles—don't settle into a single version of themselves—**until they are witnessed.**[2,3]

Let's pause here for a moment. What are the implications of the double-slit experiment?

First, it's important to recognize that this isn't fringe science. The double-slit experiment is one of the most repeated and verified experiments in modern physics—performed thousands of times, always with the same astonishing result.

Second, that result of the experiment is clear: Consciousness has a direct effect on the behavior of matter. Whether it's electrons, atoms, or even large molecules, the presence of an observer changes the outcome. Observation alters reality.

Third, CR takes this further. It proposes that this isn't just a quirk of the quantum world—it's a foundational principle. The same force that collapses a wave into a particle is active in your everyday life. Consciousness doesn't just shape subatomic particles—it shapes your reality, moment by moment, frame by frame.

As we'll explore in later chapters, observation collapses possibility into a single lived reality—and the shape that reality takes reflects the frequency of your awareness *in that exact moment.*

Before being observed, the photon isn't a particle at all—it's a *wave of potential.*
     A map of paths it *could* take.
     But once you look?
     It chooses.
     The wave pattern collapses.
     And the outcome becomes real.
     Watching changes reality.

So light is not just energy.

It's responsive. Aware of your awareness.

Everything around you is made of these same particles.

So the universe, it seems, is not something we simply *look at.*

It's something that looks back—and reshapes itself in response.

It is not waiting to be seen.

It is waiting for *you* to decide what it becomes.

In chapter 1 we saw that time bends with awareness.
Now we see that **matter** does too.

In this framework, consciousness isn't just watching the show.
It's the projector—choosing the frame and stitching it into what we call *reality*.

Reality is like a film reel with infinite frames—a wave pattern of pure possibility.
Each frame holds a different outcome—a different version of the world.
They all exist, overlapping, waiting.
But when you look, you choose.
Your awareness selects a single frame—and that becomes your world.
Just like when Light was observed.

You hit *play* on a single possibility. That act of seeing doesn't just reveal a moment in time—it writes it.

Here's an everyday example:

Imagine standing in front of a menu at a café.
There are dozens of options—each one a potential future. A muffin leads to one timeline. The smoothie, another. Maybe you sit inside. Maybe you take it to go. Each small decision spins reality in a new direction.

But you don't live them all.

You choose.

And in that moment, the wave of possibilities collapses into a single frame—one unfolding of the day. The others vanish . . . unplayed.

You don't just pass through that moment.
You shape it—by looking, by deciding, by being aware.

That's quantum mechanics—applied to consciousness.

Think of it like pulling a thread from an invisible tangled ball of infinite yarn.

The moment you pull, that thread becomes visible—real.

The rest stays hidden—until you choose again.

THE MYSTERY AT THE CORE
This brings us to a central insight in CR.

Matter is not the foundation of the universe. Consciousness is.

Why?

Because matter doesn't take form until it is observed. The building blocks of reality exist as probability waves until awareness interacts with them. Only then do they "choose" a state. Only then do they become real.

This flips the traditional model of physics upside down.

We don't live in a world where consciousness emerges *from* matter.

We live in a world where matter emerges *through* consciousness.

It's not that your brain creates awareness.

It's that awareness creates the conditions for a brain to exist at all.

Everything you call real—every sound, color, object, and thought— appears only after consciousness collapses the wave into form.

Without observation, there is no event. No particle. No time. No place.

What we call reality is what awareness chooses to see.

John Wheeler—physicist, mentor to Richard Feynman, and the man who coined the term "black hole"—believed we live in a **participatory universe**. In this view the observer isn't a passive witness. They're the final ingredient in creation itself.

Wheeler's insight affirms what the quantum experiments imply:

The act of observation is not the end of the process—it is the beginning.

Similarly, in CR, consciousness is not a by-product of the universe.

It is the architect of it.

The thread that pulls the frame.

The witness that collapses the wave.

The projector that animates reality itself.

Imagine walking through a forest covered in mist.
    You carry a lantern—your awareness.
    With each step the light reveals more of the path ahead.
    Matter manifests and organizes. Trees take shape, the ground in front of you solidifies.

The forest takes shape—but only where the light touches.

Behind you the trail fades back into fog.

There is no fixed path. Nothing is permanently "there" unless your awareness has passed through it.

The forest was always infinite—like the wave of possibility in quantum physics.

But you never see all of it at once.

You only see the part your awareness chooses—moment by moment.

This is what the collapse of possibility feels like.

You are not moving through time like a passenger on a train, watching fixed scenery pass by your window. Time isn't something prewritten that you're simply riding through.

Instead, you are revealing time—step by step—with your attention.

Each moment you experience isn't handed to you from some cosmic schedule.

It appears when you arrive. Your awareness is the spotlight that makes the moment real.

Time is not a river flowing past you, carrying you along.

It's more like a trail through tall grass—there's no clear path until you walk it.

Each step you take presses the grass down, leaving a trail behind you. That trail is your past.

But ahead of you? It's open. Undefined. Waiting.

Time doesn't exist until you light it up with your awareness.

And reality isn't sitting there, fully built, waiting for you to catch up.

It's assembled the instant you arrive, shaped by the quality of your awareness in that moment.

In this view the future is not a destination.

It's a construction site.

And consciousness is the builder.

We've explored how consciousness doesn't move *through* time—it constructs it. But time is only one part of the illusion.

What about space? What about separation?

If awareness collapses time, could it also bridge distance? Could it reveal that the boundaries between us—between things—aren't as solid as they seem?

Let's now go deeper.

ENTANGLEMENT—THE MIRROR BEYOND SPACE

Everything we call real is made of things
that cannot be regarded as real.
—NIELS BOHR, NOBEL PRIZE–WINNING PHYSICIST
AND PIONEER OF QUANTUM THEORY

What if the universe were not a vast expanse of isolated objects but a single, breathing organism, its every part inseparably linked to the whole?

This idea isn't new. For centuries, mystics, sages, and spiritual traditions around the world have pointed to the same truth:

- In **Hinduism** the concept of *Brahman* describes a unified field of existence—an eternal, boundless reality in which all things are one.
- In **Buddhism** the teaching of *interdependence* (*pratītyasamutpāda*) tells us that nothing exists independently; all phenomena arise together, coarising like waves in the same ocean.
- In **Christian mysticism** the teachings of Jesus and the writings of mystics such as Meister Eckhart point inward rather than outward. "The kingdom of heaven is within you," Jesus said— a radical statement that suggests divinity is not distant or external but something already alive inside us. Eckhart echoed this when he wrote, "The eye with which I see God is the same eye with which God sees me." At its core this tradition whispers the same truth: There is no separation between God and creation.
- In **Indigenous traditions**, from the Hopi to the Aborigines, the world is often seen as a sacred web—humans, animals, land, sky, and spirit all interconnected in a great circle of being.

And in the realm of **psychedelic experience**, countless explorers— through psilocybin, ayahuasca, and Dimethyltryptamine (DMT, a hallucinogenic drug that occurs naturally in various plants)—report the same core insight: The boundaries dissolve. The self expands. And what's left is union.

Not metaphorical union but a *felt* knowing that all is one energy, one awareness, one being wearing many faces. From deep meditation to spontaneous mystical experience, people across time and culture have reached this same truth from different paths:

That separation is an illusion. And that at the deepest level, we are not many.

We are one.

Quantum entanglement dares us to confront this idea, not as metaphor but as fact.

SPOOKY ACTION, PROVEN REAL

In the quantum world, particles can become entangled, which means they are born from the same quantum event and bound by a connection so deep that even vast distance cannot separate them.

Send these particles to opposite sides of the universe.

Now observe one.

The *moment* you do, the other—no matter how far away—*instantly* reflects the same effect of observation.

There is no delay. The effect is instantaneous.

This stunned physicists.

According to Einstein's relativity, **nothing can travel faster than light**. So how could this be happening? Information needs time to travel from one particle to the other, yet no signal or information seemed to pass between them.

Einstein called it **spooky action at a distance**.

Experiments—culminating in the Bell tests of the 1980s and repeatedly confirmed in the twenty-first century—proved that entanglement is real.[4]

Today, quantum entanglement powers cutting-edge encryption and communication, linking satellites, submarines, and secure networks across the globe.[5]

The particles behave as if the distance itself doesn't exist between them.

But what is this connection? How does it work? And perhaps more importantly, *what does it mean?*

ONE FIELD, MANY FACES

Entangled particles can be far apart in space, yet they behave as if they're still part of the same thing.

So how can that be?

Imagine wearing wireless earbuds.
One is in your left ear; the other is in your right.

Now picture playing a song—**one song heard instantly in both ears**.

If the song changes, both earbuds reflect the change at the same time. You don't think one earbud is "telling" the other what to play— they're both connected to **the same source.**

The earbuds could be on opposite sides of the planet, yet the sound shifts instantly in both.

Entangled particles behave the same way.
They don't need to "send" information across space.
They are already linked **to the same underlying source.**

They aren't two separate things.
    They're two versions of the same deeper reality, appearing in different places.

Entanglement is evidence of an underlying, unifying field that connects objects across *any* distance.

But entanglement isn't confined to particles. CR proposes it also extends to the mind itself.

If consciousness is the fundamental field—the substrate from which matter arises—then thoughts, emotions, intuitions, and even dreams are not isolated sparks inside separate skulls. They are waves in a shared field.

Frequencies.
Patterns.
Potentialities waiting to be collapsed into form.

Just like photons, your thoughts may exist in a cloud of possibility until you give attention to one. Your attention collapses the wave. And just as particles entangle, so, too, may thoughts, insights, and even entire paradigms.

Ever thought about someone and then they call you right at that moment?

Two people having the same idea at the same time is not coincidence.

History is filled with "simultaneous discoveries"—a phenomenon so common, it has a scientific name: **multiple independent discovery**.

- **Thomas Edison** and **Joseph Swan** invented the light bulb—across the Atlantic Ocean from each other, *independently*.
- **Charles Darwin** and **Alfred Russel Wallace** proposed the evolutionary theory in the same moment.
- **Isaac Newton** and **Gottfried Wilhelm Leibniz** developed calculus—independently yet at the same time.
- **Alexander Graham Bell** and **Elisha Gray** filed telephone patents *on the same day*.

This is not because one copied the other but because both tuned into the same mental wavelength—**the same underlying source**.

They're glimpses of a shared mental field—one that entangles minds just as particles do. The idea didn't come from either individual. It emerged from the field. And when the frequency was strong enough, multiple people "picked up the signal."

This idea is echoed by some of history's greatest minds.

- **Nikola Tesla** said his inventions arrived fully formed in flashes of vision.
- **Srinivasa Ramanujan**, the Indian mathematician, claimed his equations were shown to him by a goddess in dreams.
- **Thomas Edison** famously napped with a metal ball in hand and a notebook in his lap so that when he slipped into the twilight state between sleep and waking, he could catch the ideas that surfaced from the subconscious field.

The CR view suggests the following:

Your mind is not a sealed vault. It is a receiver tuned to a collective consciousness. And every thought you "have" is part of a larger wave—one that others can feel, respond to, amplify, or even help collapse into form.

This is why déjà vu, synchronicity, sudden knowing, or shared dreams aren't just oddities. They're echoes—evidence that beneath the illusion of separateness, something deeper is shared.

But what is this "something deeper"?

What are we tuning into?

THE AKASHIC FIELD: A COSMIC MEMORY GRID

Throughout history many have described this deeper field in poetic and spiritual terms—something ancient, intelligent, and aware.

One of the most enduring names for it is the **Akasha**.

Some traditions call this field the **Akashic records**—a kind of vibrational library that contains every thought, word, feeling, and event that has ever happened or *could* happen. It isn't stored in time but beyond it. It isn't written in language but in resonance. Modern mystics, seers, and intuitives have long claimed access to this field—"reading" the Akasha to glimpse possible futures, karmic imprints, or hidden knowledge.

And curiously, this idea aligns with what some quantum theorists have begun to suggest: *that information is never lost.*

That **everything that has ever existed** leaves a trace in the underlying field.

Could this be what some are unconsciously tapping into during moments of creative genius, prophetic dreams, or sudden knowing? In this light the Akashic Field isn't just mystical metaphor. It may be a kind of *higher bandwidth*—a state of elevated awareness, possibly linked to higher brain wave frequencies such as gamma (which we'll explore later).

Perhaps you are a node in a cosmic memory network—transmitting, retrieving, and entangling with the whole.

From this view:

- **Telepathy** is not supernatural. It is the native language of a shared, conscious field.
- **Collective evolution** is not linear. It unfolds through quantum entanglement—accelerated by individual awakening. As Ralph Waldo Emerson suggested, the progress of one soul is the progress of all.

You are not thinking alone.

You are not creating alone.

You are not remembering alone.

You are a tuning fork in the universal field, echoing the silent chord of the cosmos.

And the more coherent your awareness becomes, the more clearly you hear the song.

When two minds enter coherence, such as in shared meditation, love, or flow, they begin to reflect each other not just emotionally but electrically. Entrainment happens. Brain waves begin to sync. Thought becomes resonance.

But if everything is connected through this hidden field, then the boundary between the observer and the observed begins to blur.

WHAT IS THE HIDDEN FIELD?

CR challenges our classical way of thinking. In traditional science the observer stands outside reality, like a spectator in a theater, watching events unfold. But in quantum physics, that's no longer possible.

When you observe a quantum particle, you don't just see what it was doing.

Your act of observing changes what it becomes (remember Light behaving as either a wave or particle depending on observation).

That means you, the observer, are already **part of the system.**

You're not outside the universe looking in.

You must be considered as part of **the equation**, shaping the reality that unfolds.

That's why entangled particles behave as one.
It's not that they're sending signals to each other.
It's that they're both part of the same deeper field of awareness.

In CR we call this deeper layer the **CORE field**—the *Consciousness Originating Reality Engine.* It's a single, continuous field from which all matter, energy, and perception arise.

This CORE isn't made of particles. It's what particles emerge *from.* You can't touch it like a rock, but you can measure its effects—like how entangled particles stay connected no matter the distance.

Think of it like the surface of a massive ocean. Drop two pebbles far apart, and their ripples may seem separate. But zoom out, and you see—it's all the same water.

When we investigate the quantum world, we're seeing the outlines of a deeper architecture—a field that links all things.

Every particle, every moment, every observer is a ripple in this shared field, not separate but individually expressed.

It's the single source from which all perspectives emerge.

Now let's take it further. Imagine reality as a giant mirror ball suspended in the dark. Each of us is a mirrored tile on its surface, reflecting the world from a unique angle. But the light that hits all of us—that illuminates the ball and all reality, the source we reflect—is one and the same.

From this view entanglement doesn't violate causality. It reveals something deeper: a hidden layer where all division disappears, and what we call separate is just the illusion of separation placed on top of unity.

We all are truly one.

Not many minds collapsing separate realities but one shared awareness shaping one coherent world, viewed from many windows.

WHO—OR WHAT—IS THE OBSERVER?

*No phenomenon is a phenomenon until
it is an observed phenomenon.*
—JOHN ARCHIBALD WHEELER, THEORETICAL PHYSICIST

Let's pause and gather what we've uncovered so far.

The **double-slit experiment** shattered the idea of an objective, ob-
server-independent world—showing that matter doesn't take form
until it is seen.

Entanglement cracked open our assumptions about space, time, and
individuality—revealing that what appears separate may still be part
of the same deeper whole.

We've seen that matter is not the foundation of reality—*consciousness is.*
And that consciousness doesn't merely witness reality—it selects the
frame.

From that selection, matter emerges, not randomly but from a deeper
source we call the CORE.

CORE is the field of consciousness that weaves all of existence together—a shared source from which all observers draw their reality
and into which all experiences return.

This isn't philosophy dressed up in science.

It's a new lens for understanding reality—one that places you not at the edge of the universe looking in but at the *center of the unfolding.*

But it does more than that.

It hints at a greater self—not a character trapped inside the simulation but the one writing the code.

CR proposes a reversal of the standard model.
    Consciousness isn't a by-product of the brain.
    It's the field that gives rise to the brain—and the world—by collapsing potential into form.

Just as a photon becomes a particle only when observed, your body, your life—your sense of self—only takes shape when consciousness engages with it.

Imagine reality as an infinite radio spectrum.
    Each possibility—every thought, identity, or moment—is a frequency on that dial.
    The brain isn't the broadcaster.
    It's the receiver, tuning into whatever station consciousness selects.

This suggests the observer isn't a person but a position—a point of view inside the CORE.

That field may be vast.
    It may extend beyond the boundary of personal memory and even beyond time.

Many wisdom traditions speak of this deeper observer as timeless.

The Upanishads call it the Atman—the Self behind all selves.

Buddhist philosophy speaks of it as pure awareness, untouched by thought.

In Christian mysticism it is the "I AM" that Moses encounters at the burning bush—the being itself.

Who collapses the wave?
Who receives the echo?
Who peers into the mirror of space and time—and sees itself reflected in everything?

And in the next section, we'll begin tracing this observer back to its source—not as a person, not even as a mind, but as the silent eye behind all becoming.

Imagine a stained glass window.
As sunlight shines through, the colors shift depending on the glass, but the light behind it never changes.

Each of us is a unique window.
Different shapes, shades, and patterns.

But the light that shines through us—the capacity to be aware, to choose, to witness—is something that existed *before the glass*.

The observer is not the pattern on the window.
The observer is *the light passing through it*.

This is why in near-death experiences, deep meditation, or psychedelic states, people often report "becoming the light" or "merging with everything." The stained glass drops away, and only the light remains. The awareness witnessing it all—without edges, without identity—becomes visible to itself.

COLLECTIVE OBSERVATION
But a new question arises:

If each observer collapses reality through awareness, *why does the world remain consistent for all of us?*

Why don't we each see entirely separate realities?

If collapse happens from within, why does the tree remain fallen even after the last person walks away?

ONE COLLAPSE, SEEN FROM MANY ANGLES
Collapse appears to happen locally—inside one person's experience.
But it follows a logic that feels *shared*, as if seeing the same event from a slightly different angle.

Like sunlight shining through many windows, each casting a unique multicolored beam yet all coming from the same source.

This is the paradox.

The observer feels personal.
But the pattern it tunes into seems universal.

And so CR proposes a quiet but powerful idea:

There are not many observers. There is one CORE—appearing through many eyes.
Like gravity or electricity, this field also has a force.
But its force is not physical.
Its force is awareness.

Wherever awareness shows up, the field activates.
Wherever you focus, possibility turns into something real.

NOT A FRAGMENT BUT A FACET
This changes how we understand individuality.

You are not a fragment, broken off from something greater.
That would imply separation.

You are a window—one shape, one view—lit by the same light source as every other.

Like a **single cell** that carries the code of the whole body.
　　Like a **mirror piece** that still reflects the whole image.
　　Like a **wave rising from a vast ocean**—different in shape, same in source.

And just as waves influence one another, your ripples affect the entire field. Your attention, your emotional tone, your frequency—these shape not just your reality but the shared reality. This insight forms the heart of karma, not as punishment but as vibrational echo. What you collapse into the world rebounds back to you.

While we all share the same light, each of us puts our own spin on it, shaping it through our unique lens.

We are not many creators constructing many worlds.
We are **one field collapsing one world experience—together.**

This is why the world feels coherent, even though awareness is spread across all of us.

Each viewpoint shapes the unfolding. But the field holds it all in harmony. The coordination isn't forced—it's emergent. Like birds flying in formation, no one is leading, but everyone is aligned.

Collapse happens individually, but the possibilities we each draw from are shaped by the same field, ensuring harmony over chaos.

THE SYMPHONY OF PERCEPTION

When one person observes, collapse happens.
A possibility becomes a reality—a frame locks into place.

But when many observe, something extraordinary occurs:

Collapse becomes *coordinated*.
Reality starts to harmonize across perspectives.

Each observer tunes into the world from their own seat at the cosmic concert.

Yet somehow the melody remains the same.
Not because we all play *identical* notes but because we're tuning into the **same underlying song**.

Like musicians in an orchestra—each hearing something slightly different yet all playing from one shared score.

We are not individual soloists playing disconnected songs.
We are instruments tuned to one cosmic key.
Each life is a variation on a theme.
Each perception is a note in a grander score.
And while we may not always recognize the melody, we are playing it, together.

This is how entanglement spans galaxies.
How particles sync across space with no signal.
How our memory of the world still matches, even though we've lived entirely different lives.

We see hints of this even at the largest scales.

Images from modern space telescopes reveal the **cosmic web**—a vast, threadlike structure of galaxies and dark matter spanning the universe.

It looks strikingly like a neural network or the filaments of a living brain.

EXHIBIT 2A

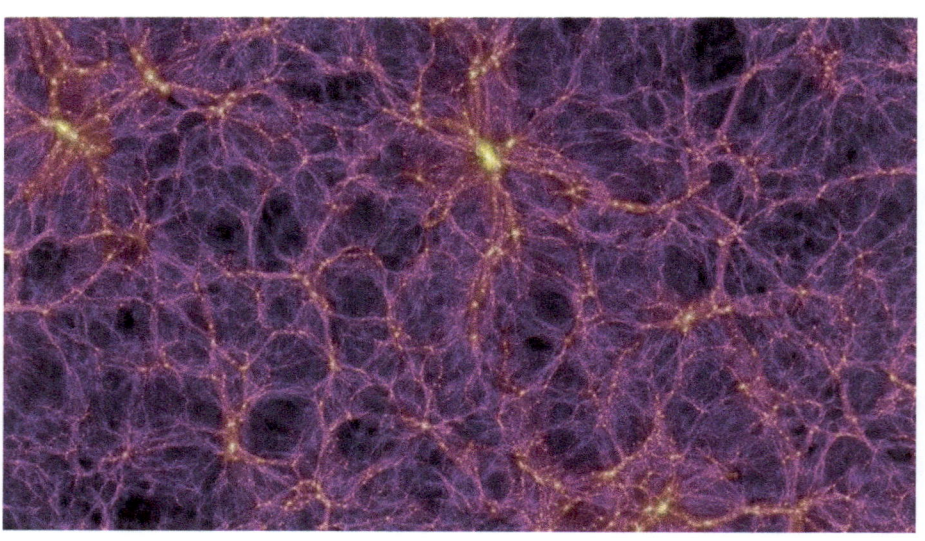

Above: A visualization of the cosmic web from the James Webb Space Telescope. Though it maps galaxies across billions of light-years, its structure mirrors that of the human brain's neural network, suggesting a universal architecture of connection.

Just as the cosmic web illustrates the universe's large-scale structure, our brain's neural networks reflect a similar intricate connectivity. This mirroring suggests a fundamental pattern of interconnectedness, from the vastness of space to the depths of human consciousness.

Science sees gravity.

CR sees something more:

A visible echo of consciousness—a physical mirror of the CORE.

Awareness taking shape as structure, spanning the cosmos like thoughts span the mind.

It's how we can dream alone but wake into a world that continues without us, as if someone else had been "holding the frame" for us as we slept.

This isn't mysticism.

It aligns with the verified results of the quantum world.

- **Collapse is local**—It happens inside your awareness, the moment you observe or make a choice. A wave of possibility becomes a single, lived outcome.
- **But the logic behind collapse is global**—It is as if one silent conductor guides every hand, ensuring that each local experience still harmonizes with the larger unfolding.

This global synchrony—what CR calls the CORE—is what allows individual awareness to remain in step with the larger composition.

The beauty is we are never truly alone.

All consciousness is entangled—held in harmony by something deeper than thought.

Which means that **compassion toward one another isn't just moral.**

It's logical.

WHEN AWARENESS TOUCHES THE INFINITE

We've followed the trail of quantum mystery—where light behaves like possibility, where matter doesn't exist until it's seen, and where even galaxies apart, particles remain connected as one.

We've turned inward—past the body, the brain, and the idea of a separate self—until only a field of shared awareness remained.

But one question still lingers:

If consciousness turns potential into reality—and all reality unfolds in time—then what exactly *is* time? And if, as Einstein showed, time bends with motion, what happens when it bends with awareness?

THE STITCHED ILLUSION REVISITED

In chapter 1 Einstein showed us that time bends with speed and gravity.

CR now shows us that time bends with awareness.

In this model, time is not stretched—it is selected.

Not something we move through but something that emerges as we collapse the possibilities.

Each moment is a choice among infinite potential.

Each "now" is a frame pulled from all the possibilities into focus— *and sculpted in real time by the vibrational tone of the awareness choosing it.*

But how *clearly* we collapse these frames depends on our state of awareness.

In CR we associate these awareness levels with measurable brain wave patterns—something we'll explore more deeply in later chapters.

- **Lower awareness**, often paired with slower brain wave states such as theta or low alpha brain waves, means less clarity, less presence.
- **Higher awareness**, linked to faster, more coherent brain waves such as gamma, leads to sharper perception and fuller moments.

Consider this:

You're driving home on autopilot, your mind elsewhere.

You pull into your driveway, turn off the engine, and realize you barely remember the ride.

The frames collapsed but without presence.

Time moved, but nothing felt *real*—you skimmed across the surface.

Now contrast that with a moment of deep presence: watching the Sun sink behind the ocean or holding eye contact with someone you love.

You're fully engaged.

Each frame becomes richer, denser, more alive.

It's not that time *stretches*.

It's that you *enter* the moment more fully.

The difference isn't in how long the moment lasted but in how fully you collapsed it into reality.

At lower states of awareness—when you're distracted by your phone, mindlessly scrolling social media—you're collapsing frames but not absorbing them, just skimming the surface.

- Frame selection is **reactive**, **unconscious**, driven by habit, emotion, or external noise.
- Like flipping channels without noticing what's playing.
- You collapse frames rapidly—reactively—without coherence or intention. You're skimming reality, not shaping it.

Your awareness flits from one frame to the next—jumpy, shallow, fragmented.

Hours pass, but nothing truly registers.

You look up, and the day is gone.

You were "there," but you didn't *feel* there.

Time flowed past you, not through you.

At higher states of awareness—like when you're fully present during a sunset, locked in creative flow, or listening deeply to someone you love—you **enter** the frames. Each one becomes dense, vivid, luminous—like time stretching to make room for the depth of your presence.

You're not flipping through reality. You're inside it.

- Frame selection is **deliberate**, **attuned**, guided by inner coherence or purpose.
- Like a director choosing the perfect shot, not just what's next but what *matters*.
- Each frame is selected with care, meaning you draw more reality from collapses.

Time seems to slow down.

A single moment deepens, becoming wide with detail and weight.

You notice details: the shape of a cloud, the pause in someone's breath, the way light touches a surface.

Your thoughts quiet, and something opens.

You don't just experience more per frame—you also **choose** your frames more deliberately. Awareness becomes a steady spotlight.

You don't just experience time—you *shape* it. Like a single moment with a loved one that somehow holds a lifetime. In these moments it's not the clock that changes.

It's the precision of the collapse.

You're selecting frames more deliberately—more consciously—and that changes how long a moment feels and how real it becomes.

This shift in awareness reshapes the very rhythm of collapse. Time doesn't just feel different—it *forms* differently. A moment becomes fuller, slower, realer, not because the clock changed but because **you did**.

At the highest awareness levels, collapse is intentional and expansive, time becomes *malleable*, just as in Einstein's physics.

Your chosen frame reshapes not just the now but your sense of what led there.

At higher levels of awareness, the present becomes so rich—so densely packed with meaning—that it begins to bend backward. It casts light on the path behind you.

You don't just change what's next.

You *reorganize* what came before.

Memory is not a static record—it's a reconstruction, and the mind builds it around the present moment you've collapsed. That means the deeper your awareness in *this* moment, the more clearly the story behind it comes into focus.

Details you once missed become visible.
Connections you hadn't seen now snap into place.

It feels like you're remembering more, but you're actually perceiving more. The moment you choose doesn't just shape your future. It rethreads your past. The now becomes the anchor, and from it, your mind weaves the story in both directions. This is why a single moment of insight, forgiveness, or presence can reframe an entire lifetime.

Because the frame you collapse now becomes the one that defines the story you tell about how you got here.

At lower awareness, you ride the train of time, watching scenes fly past the window—passenger to a journey you don't remember boarding, headed to a destination you didn't choose.

At higher awareness, you're the conductor—able to slow it down, switch tracks, even **rewrite what the last station looked like**.

SHAPING THE INFINITE

In ordinary states awareness moves quickly, collapsing frame after frame in rapid-fire succession—like flipping through a photo reel too quickly to see what's in each image.

This is what we call **normal time**—a steady stream of seconds, marching forward in order. Linear. Predictable. Measurable.

But something different happens in altered states—whether through deep meditation, trauma, revelation, or near-death experiences.

Time suddenly opens.

You may have felt this in moments you couldn't explain.

- The breathless stillness before holding your child for the first time
- A moment of prayer or meditation when the world fell away
- The frozen eternity during a car accident
- The expansion of self during a psychedelic or spiritual experience
- A recurring childhood trauma that loops throughout life

These aren't hallucinations.

They are temporary pauses in the frame-by-frame construction of reality.

When awareness reaches such an elevated state, it is no longer selecting. It slips between the frames—and shapes the field of the infinite.

Time then isn't a river we ride—it's a trail we leave behind as we move through choice.

TIME DOESN'T SHRINK—AWARENESS EXPANDS

Here's the paradox:

The deeper your awareness, the **more fully you experience** a moment.

It's not that "less time passes."
   It's that **you experience more within the same amount of time**.

- In low awareness sixty seconds feels like background noise.
- In heightened awareness sixty seconds can feel endless and full.

This isn't poetic. It's measurable, as we'll see in later chapters.
   Your brain literally processes and integrates more detail per moment at higher frequencies.

That's why time feels slower during trauma, creative flow, or moments of deep insight, not because more frames are collapsed but because **each frame carries more experience**. In high-frequency brain states such as gamma, this becomes measurable: Awareness integrates more emotion, detail, and presence **into each selected frame**.

Each frame becomes *thicker* with meaning, not longer in duration but deeper in what it holds.

This creates what CR calls **internal time dilation**—a subjective slowing of time caused not by speed or gravity but by the depth of awareness.

You've felt it before.

Imagine you're sitting on the floor with a young child.
Blocks scatter. Toys tumble. They laugh.
And something in that sound catches you.

The laugh is light and pure. Timeless.
You look up, and suddenly, you're not thinking about your to-do list or your phone or the next hour.
You're just *there.*
Every color sharpens.
Every sound feels like part of a song.
Time, for a moment, forgets to move.

That's internal time dilation—your awareness rising, your presence deepening.
One moment expands to hold more life than usual.

Einstein taught us that time slows when you move faster through space.
But here, it's not speed—it's *awareness* that bends the clock.

The child's laughter—like a photon—was always there in potential.
But it became fully real only when you collapsed into the moment.
Until then, it was just background.

That shared glance, that ripple of joy—that's entanglement.
Not a metaphor but a *felt truth*: two beings, linked through presence, experiencing one reality across two minds.

And behind it all: the CORE.
The field of consciousness holding this moment open.
The laugh. The light. The meaning.
One field, two perspectives.
One world, infinitely framed.

You didn't just witness this moment.
You made it real.

One frame.
One now.
Infinite joy, collapsed into form.

Like relativity—where time slows for an object moving near the speed of light—awareness creates its own dilation. But instead of velocity, it's consciousness that bends the clock.

You don't need to rush through ten moments to find meaning in one. You're already in the one that matters.

In these states time doesn't disappear—it just becomes irrelevant. Awareness grows so full, so present that time fades into stillness. There is only now.

You're no longer watching the film.
 You are the projector—casting light through the reel of possibility, choosing the story that becomes real.

In this chapter we've stepped into a reality stranger than fiction—where observation brings the world into being, where objects separated across any distance are still one, and where your awareness is not inside time but the source from which time flows.

Light does not become a particle until you look.
Time does not unfold until you choose.
And you are not watching the story.
You are the lens through which the story becomes real.

In chapter 3 we begin tuning the instrument of reality, exploring how vibration sculpts space, how sound gives rise to structure, and how the universe sings itself into form.

RECAP: CHAPTER 2: THE CONSCIOUS ARCHITECT

We began with a particle of light—a photon—choosing its path only when observed.

And we ended with awareness itself bending time, collapsing potential into experience.

In this chapter we explored the quantum riddles that point to something extraordinary:

- **Reality does not exist in a fixed form.** It emerges when consciousness observes it—when the wave becomes a particle, when possibility becomes presence.
- **Entangled particles** behave as one across any distance, not because they're sending signals but because they never stopped being one. Separation is the illusion.
- **Your thoughts,** like photons, exist in a cloud of possibility—until you collapse one through attention.
- **Minds,** too, may be entangled. Shared ideas, synchronicity, déjà vu, and sudden inspiration aren't coincidences. They're echoes of a unified field.
- **You are not a sealed container of awareness.** You are a tuning fork in the cosmic field—a lens through which the universe observes itself.

- **The observer isn't your personality or memory.** It is the silent witness behind the eyes—the field of awareness itself. And that field is shared.
- **Reality appears stable because we are many facets of one awareness**—collapsing the world into coherence through countless angles of perception.
- **Time, too, is not fixed.** It flows at the rhythm of collapse. At low awareness it flickers by. At high awareness it deepens. And in the deepest presence, time dissolves completely.

3

THE SCULPTOR OF FORM

In the beginning was the Word, and the Word
was with God, and the Word was God.
—JOHN 1:1, KING JAMES VERSION

SOUND BEFORE LIGHT: THE SCULPTOR OF FORM

The ship has returned from Saturn. The journey stretched far beyond planets and time.

The crew touched the edges of reality—where time loosened, space shimmered, and consciousness became the only true compass. Though only **one hour** passed on board, **a thousand years** had unfolded back on Earth. That was the cost—and the miracle—of traveling near light speed. Einstein had shown them the truth: Time is not absolute. It bends.

But the Saturn mission did more than bend time.

It folded space itself, not with engines but with intention. The ship rode waves of probability, collapsing each moment like stepping stones ahead of them. They had used **quantum mechanics** not as a theory but as a *technology*—one that treated space and time not as separate threads but as a single fabric that could be tuned.

And what tuned it wasn't mass or force.

It was something more subtle, more fundamental.

In chapter 2 we explored how the observer selects from infinite possibility, collapsing a wave of potential into one frame of now that emerges from the CORE field.

But once a frame is chosen, how does it gain structure? How does it become a world of form, texture, and meaning?

The answer is **vibration**.

And from this vibration, sound.

The ancients knew this.

Across cultures and ages, nearly every creation story begins not with light but with a sound. A voice. A breath.

Let there be light. Om. Logos. The Word. The Breath.

Vibration is what gives shape to the formless—the invisible sculptor that arranges the chaos of space into structure.

Picture a still pond.

Drop a pebble, and ripples expand outward.

Drop several pebbles in harmony, and patterns emerge—interference, geometry, symmetry.

But if the timing is off, the water turns chaotic.

Now imagine the pond is not water but the **fabric of reality itself**.

Every thought, every sound, every pulse of awareness sends vibrations into that field.

At lower frequencies the patterns are broad and blunt—slow waves, simple forms.

But as the frequency rises, the patterns become more intricate.

Sharper.

Alive with order.

This is the nature of vibration.

Not just movement through space but **structure emerging from rhythm**.

Not just sound but **sound becoming shape**.

This isn't just poetry—it's physics.

It's called *cymatics*—the study of how sound and vibration shape physical matter (literally "the scientific study of wave phenomena").

SOUND SHAPES SAND—VIBRATION SHAPES LIFE

Cymatics reveals what was once hidden. When sound passes through a surface—sand, water, metal—it leaves a visible signature. It draws order from silence. Order is born from vibration. Chaos crystallizes into beauty.

In cymatic experiments, sound becomes visible. A simple experiment involves placing a metal plate over a speaker and sprinkling it with fine sand. As a tone plays from the speaker, it vibrates the plate, and the sand leaps into geometric order, forming stars, spirals, and mandalas. Change the frequency, and the pattern shifts. The higher the frequency, the finer the form. Lower it, and it simplifies.

- At lower frequencies (e.g., 100 Hz) the form might yield simple, crude shapes or clumps.
- At 1,000 Hz we see intricate lacework—symmetry, geometry, and elegance.

EXHIBIT 3A

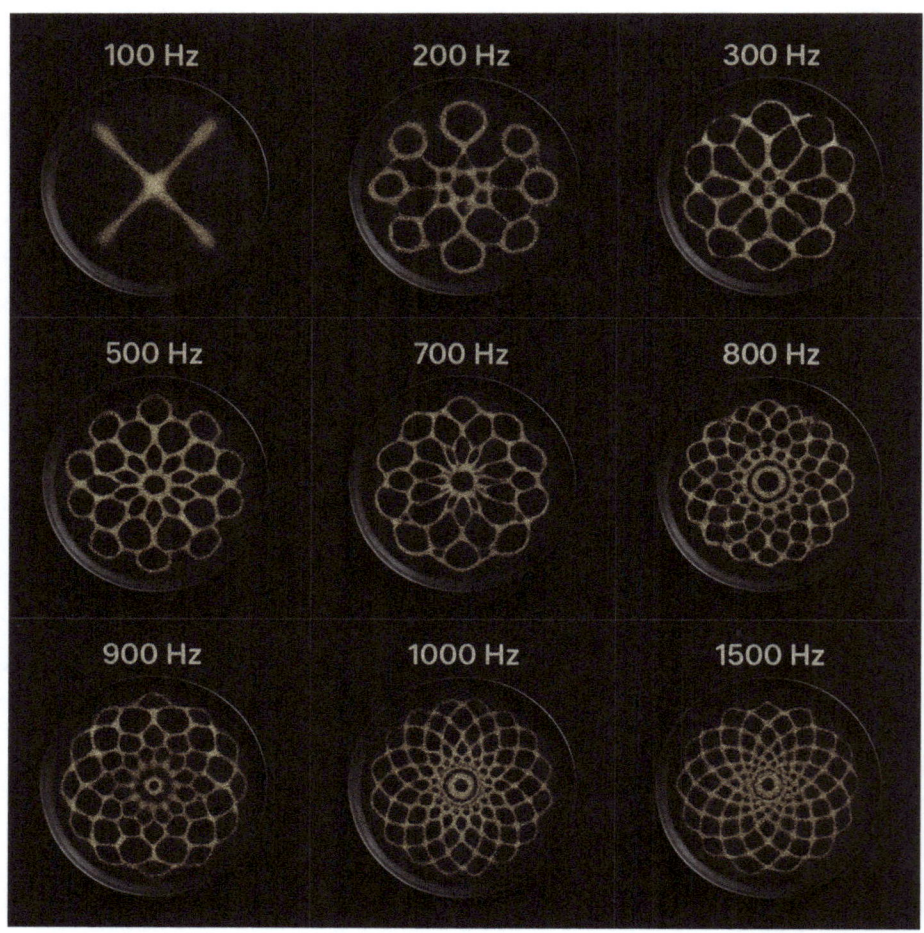

Above: Illustrative sand on a metal plate vibrated by a tone generator (cymascope). As the frequency increases, the patterns become more intricate and refined. In the same way, higher states of consciousness—expressed through elevated internal frequency—generate more harmonious, complex, and beautiful experiences in life.

Cymatics is scientific evidence that sound doesn't just move through matter—it tells it what to become.

In the documentary *Inner Worlds, Outer Worlds*, a striking experiment is shown where corn syrup is poured into a bowl of water, then exposed to different frequencies. At certain tones the mixture begins to swirl, pulse, and organize, as if animated from within. It looks alive.

But nothing was added. No biology. No program. Just vibration.

Modern physics, too, has begun to echo this truth.

String theory proposes that the fundamental building blocks of the universe are not particles but **vibrating strings of energy**. Each type of particle—from photons to quarks—arises not from different matter but from different frequencies.

These strings don't play in visible space alone. They ripple through **hidden dimensions**, unseen layers of reality curled into the quantum fabric. Much like a harp string resonates beyond its visible length, these cosmic filaments stretch across space-time, weaving the universe through tone.

This is today's leading scientific theory of the universe—*and it is based on vibration.*

What the ancients intuited through mantra and sacred sound, string theory now whispers in the equations of physics: **The universe did not begin with matter but with vibration**. We are made not of atoms but of rhythm.

In the next section, we'll explore how nature itself—trees, galaxies, DNA, and even your heartbeat—echoes these same harmonic patterns, revealing that vibration is not an effect of matter **but its origin**.

NATURE MIRRORS FREQUENCY: THE CYMATIC BLUEPRINT IN LIFE

If vibration sculpts sand into geometry, as cymatics shows, then we should see its imprint not just in the lab but throughout the natural world.

And we do.

All around us **life mirrors these patterns**. The same spirals, rings, and fractal patterns seen in cymatic experiments appear in galaxies, shells, flowers, and cells. This is not coincidence.

It's a **blueprint**.

A sunflower doesn't just grow.

It arranges itself in spirals that mirror the golden ratio—a mathematical harmony found in vibrating systems. A pinecone, a hurricane, a snail shell, and beehives—all unfold in logarithmic spirals, the *same geometry seen in high-frequency cymatic plates*.

Snowflakes crystallize in hexagonal symmetry, as if frozen in song. The branches of trees, the folds of your lungs, and the forking of rivers—each follow fractal algorithms, recursive vibrations shaping form with elegant precision.

Have you ever wondered why broccoli looks like a miniature tree? Why a lightning bolt splits like the veins in a leaf or the arteries in your body? Why coastlines, coral reefs, and clouds all echo the same branching forms?

These patterns are not random. They are **signatures of frequency**—expressions of a deeper order encoded into the structure of space itself. Whether in nature or the human body, form unfolds in response to underlying vibration.

You are not separate from this symmetry. You are a continuation of it.

Even your DNA—the coiled script of your body—spirals in a double helix, echoing the same patterns found throughout nature. This elegant shape isn't just a chemical convenience—it's a geometric masterpiece, *a spiral staircase of life*, built from balance and rhythm.

You see this same spiral in galaxies, hurricanes, the unfurling of ferns, and seashells. It's the curve of growth, the path of least resistance, the architecture of flow. DNA follows this same path not by accident but because life moves in resonance with natural harmony.

The double helix is a stable harmonic structure because it holds information without breaking down. It's efficient, self-reinforcing, and beautifully coherent—a cymatic form encoded into biology itself.

Its resonance is not just metaphor. Scientists are now measuring the vibrational frequencies of DNA itself. These vibrations aren't side effects—they *are* function, shaping how cells behave, communicate, and express life. DNA emits and absorbs photons at specific frequencies,[1,2] guiding cellular communication like a wireless transmitter, using light as its language. **Bio-resonance** refers to the phenomenon where biological systems communicate and regulate through these vibrational frequencies.[3] It suggests that life organizes not just through chemistry but through tone. Emerging research shows this resonance may influence everything, from protein folding to gene expression, implying that a vibrational language is woven into the fabric of life.[4]

In this light, DNA is not a static script but a singing coil—an antenna tuned to the frequency field of the body. Every cell, every function may be humming in chorus to a deeper harmony.

This makes DNA not just a code but a song—a melody broadcast through the living field.

These patterns are not passive. They are *instructions*—blueprints whispered into matter by the underlying field of reality.

This orchestration isn't confined to form—it's embedded in the very constants that govern reality.

Physicists have long recognized that the universe is not just structured but **finely tuned**. The force of gravity, the mass of subatomic particles, and the expansion rate of the cosmos—each operates within a razor-thin range. Shift any of them ever so slightly, and stars wouldn't form, chemistry couldn't stabilize, and life as we know it would never emerge.

This is known as the **fine-tuning problem**, and it suggests something profound: *that existence itself is balanced on a knife's edge of perfection.*

Some theorists invoke the concept of a **multiverse**—an infinite ensemble of parallel universes, each with different physical laws and constants. In this view we just happen to live in the one where the "dials" are set perfectly for life, because if they weren't, we wouldn't be here to observe it. This is known as the **anthropic principle**—the idea that conscious observers will always find themselves in a universe capable of producing them. The multiverse provides a kind of statistical escape hatch: Life is rare but inevitable somewhere, given infinite universes.

Others see this precision not as a cosmic lottery but as evidence of **intentional design**—a universe so exquisitely calibrated for life that it suggests underlying intelligence or purpose. From this perspective the constants of nature—gravity, electromagnetism, and the strong and weak nuclear forces—didn't fall into place by accident. They were chosen, balanced, or emerged from some deeper source of order. Whether described as God, or universal mind, this view holds that **consciousness or intelligence preceded form**, and the universe was born already in tune.

From a CR perspective, fine-tuning is not accidental or imposed—it is **inevitable in a universe where consciousness is primary**. The constants are what they are because they express the most coherent pattern possible.

Life is the natural flowering of a conscious universe humming in tune.

Just as cymatic waves organize sand into precise forms, the universe organizes itself through an unseen ordering principle—what CR calls the **entangled CORE field**. This field is not a background. It is an intelligent matrix—**woven from vibration, shaped by awareness, and shared across space and time**.

The spiral in a pine cone, the hexagon in a snowflake, and the double helix in your DNA—none of these is random. They are echoes—*echoes of a unified geometry pulsing from the CORE.*

And because this field is entangled, each part carries the whole. The same design principles that shape galaxies also shape your cells. **The same harmonics that organize stars are vibrating inside you.**

In CR, form is not imposed—it is **received**. Every leaf, every organ, every life path is a translation of frequency into structure.

It's no wonder then that these repeating shapes, found across scales and species, are part of a deeper human language.

Sacred geometry.

Sacred geometry is the art of honoring the patterns that nature repeats—circles, spirals, triangles, and stars. These shapes appear again and again, not by accident but because they reveal how harmony expresses itself in space.

These forms aren't random. They arise from harmony. We see them in the petals of flowers, the spiral of galaxies, and the structure of shells and snowflakes. They are the fingerprints of a deeper order—geometry born from vibration, symmetry shaped by sound. For thousands of years, humans have used sacred geometry in temples, art, and architecture, not just for beauty but to reflect the deep order they saw in the universe and to honor the divine. From temples to mandalas, from pyramids to stained glass windows, these patterns were woven into our art and architecture to mirror the harmony we sensed in the cosmos.

Sacred geometry is not only visual—it is also deeply numerical. Beneath the forms are ratios, measurements, and angles that reveal a hidden intelligence at work.

One of the most profound patterns is the number **9**. Across many sacred geometries, all angles—squares (360°), triangles (180°), and circles (360°)—when added as digits, reduce to 9 (3 + 6 + 0 = 9). This is not an isolated anomaly but a recurring signature. Whether in the Enneagram, the vesica piscis, or nonagon-based architecture, **9 emerges as the symbol of completion, resonance, and cosmic return.**

The number 9 is not just a digit. It's a cipher—a recursive constant that appears when things complete, when cycles close, and when patterns return to source. Multiply it, rotate it, embed it in Fibonacci spirals or musical structures—it returns unchanged. This isn't math—it's memory. Ancient systems knew this. That's why there are 9 Muses in Greek mythology, 9 spheres in Dante's *Inferno*, and 9 realms in Norse cosmos.

The number 9 marks the boundary between separation and unity. It is the tone of return.

In mathematics the number 9 behaves differently from all other digits. Multiply 9 by any number, and the digits always reduce to 9.

- $9 \times 1 = 9$
- $9 \times 2 = 18 \rightarrow 1 + 8 = 9$
- $9 \times 3 = 27 \rightarrow 2 + 7 = 9$
- $9 \times 10 = 90 \rightarrow 9 + 0 = 9$

It acts like a self-similar fractal digit—an attractor that folds back into itself. This is central to vortex-based math (popularized by Marko Rodin), where 9 is seen as the axis point of a torus, representing the "control" field of energy—what 3 and 6 spin around.

This blueprint also extends into the human body.

The average human stride length when walking is about 5.28 feet. Multiply this by 1,000 strides, and you get 5,280 feet—exactly 1 mile. Why does this matter? Because the mile, often considered an arbitrary imperial measure, encodes more than convenience. *It encodes measurement between the body and the cosmos.*

Now consider this:

- The **Moon's diameter** is approximately **2,160 miles** *(2 + 1 + 6 + 0 = 9)*.
- Multiply this by **108**, and you get **233,280 miles**—astonishingly close to the average Earth–Moon distance.
- The **Sun's diameter** is approximately **864,000 miles** *(8 + 6 + 4 = 18; 1 + 8 = 9)*.
- Multiply this by **108**, and you get **93,312,000 miles**—nearly an exact match for the average Earth–Sun distance.

In both cases **108** links the diameter of these celestial bodies to their distance from Earth. And **1 + 0 + 8 = 9**, the vibrational constant that reappears in geometry, time cycles, and spiritual systems. Some scholars and esoteric mathematicians have noted that these cosmic distances correlate with ratios embedded in human scale and measurement, including the mile, the pyramid inch, and the ancient cubit. In other words the **human gait, the mile, and the cosmos are proportionally entangled**.

It's as if the body remembers something the intellect has forgotten— that we walk within a harmonic universe, and even our pace is in step with the stars.

Culturally we even reference 9.

- **"Cloud Nine"**: Symbol of elation, bliss, or spiritual ecstasy.
- **"Dressed to the Nines"**: Meaning impeccably presented, possibly referring to being at the *peak* of elegance (i.e., 9 = peak digit).
- **Beethoven's 9th Symphony**: Often called the **symphony of the divine** and the last he completed before his death—a symbol of musical completion.

And beneath culture, myth, and math, there is the subtle intuition that 9 is not merely a number—it's a frequency of return. In Vedic numerology, it is the digit of culmination, the final cycle before rebirth. In vortex mathematics it is the still point around which all other motion spirals. Even the Fibonacci sequence, when reduced to single digits, cycles every 24 numbers—and always returns to 9. It is the silent heartbeat of wholeness, echoing across time, sound, and structure. Not the start of a journey. The home we spiral back to.

Nikola Tesla famously said, "If you only knew the magnificence of 3, 6, and 9, then you would have the key to the universe."

To Tesla, these were not just numbers—they were vibrational archetypes. In his personal journals and diagrams, 9 was the pinnacle, the number that governed energy flow, resonance, and universal design. Where 3 and 6 created motion, spiraling in and out, 9 held the axis of stillness, the silent center through which all force resolves. In this light 9 isn't just a mathematical curiosity. It's the number of the **source, CORE field**—the unseen architecture behind form, frequency, and return.

And then there is **gematria**—the ancient Hebrew system where **letters carry numeric value**, making every word a frequency code.

- The Tetragrammaton-Yod (10), Heh (5), Vav (6), and Heh (5)—the sacred four-letter name of God (הוהי / YHVH)—adds up to 26.
- 26 becomes symbolically important: In English, "God" also corresponds to G (7) + O (15) + D (4) = 26—a mirrored correspondence between two vastly different languages.
- There are 26 letters in the English alphabet.

These patterns suggest language is not merely symbolic—it is mathematical structure encoded in sound.

For millennia, sacred geometry has been revered by humanity not just as art but as a spiritual science.

Ancient cultures recognized that certain shapes and proportions carry intrinsic power from resonance. These forms echo the organizing patterns of the universe itself.

Builders believed that certain geometric ratios could **amplify divine frequency**, turning stone buildings into song.

They were instruments—**resonant chambers built to tune the soul**.

You see it in the pyramids of Egypt, built with precise angles and aligned to the stars.

In Hindu mandalas, where circles and squares reflect the layered structure of the universe.

In Gothic cathedrals, where arches, rose windows, and spires were designed using sacred geometric ratios to create spaces that resonated with spiritual energy.

These weren't just artistic choices—they were attempts to shape matter in harmony with the divine. Some sacred sites, such as **Chartres Cathedral**, are known to resonate at specific frequencies—specifically, **432 Hz**, long believed to be a harmonic of Earth's own natural resonance. In these spaces chanting or organ tones don't merely echo. They activate the entire chamber. The walls hum. The body vibrates. The architecture becomes a living instrument—**tuned to transcendence**.

The number 432 (4 + 3 + 2 = 9) appears throughout sacred tradition, geometry, and cosmology. It's encoded in the diameter of the Sun, the timing of Earth's precession, the geometry of ancient temples, and even the tuning systems of early music. Ancient cultures saw it not just as a number but as a **universal key**. The number 432 appears like a whisper from the blueprint of the universe itself. Even in number theory, its prime factorization—$2^4 \times 3^3$—reflects a balance between polarity and expansion.

- **The height of the Great Pyramid** (from base to apex, including the missing capstone) is roughly 432 cubits. Some interpretations of its inner structure and perimeter also encode 432 harmonically, especially when converted into sacred Egyptian units.
- **Stonehenge and Angkor Wat:** Researchers have noted that multiples and factors of 432 show up in the spatial layout and geometry of numerous megalithic structures. For example, the outermost sarsen circle at Stonehenge has a diameter that approximates a multiple of 432 inches.
- **The Zodiac:** $432 \times 60 = 25{,}920$ (years in a full precession of our astrological symbols, the zodiac).
- **The Vedas:** 432,000 = years in a Yuga in Vedic cosmology (a sacred measurement of time).

- **Seconds in a day:** 86,400 (seconds in a day) ÷ 2 = 43,200; also, the diameter of the Sun (864,000 miles).
- When sound is vibrated through a medium (e.g., sand on a Chladni plate, as shown above), 432 Hz produces more symmetrical and organic patterns than 440 Hz. It seems to harmonize more deeply with geometric resonance structures.

For millennia, human music was naturally attuned to this frequency. It was not until the twentieth century—specifically in 1939, under the influence of the Rockefeller Foundation and global standardization efforts—that the tuning of **music shifted from 432 Hz to 440 Hz.** Some believe this seemingly subtle shift nudged music out of alignment with natural resonance, creating a dissonance that modern ears have come to accept unconsciously.

But when we return to 432, something deep inside us remembers.

It's not just music. It's medicine.

A vibration that restores coherence, not just in the body but in the field.

The architects of Chartres and Chartres-like structures weren't just constructing churches. They were embedding vibration into form—layering proportions based on the golden ratio, Fibonacci sequences, and Platonic solids—in an effort to bring matter into alignment with the vibration of the CORE field.

You see echoes of this in Notre-Dame de Paris, whose rose windows are based on intricate radial symmetry and whose layout follows precise geometric ratios meant to mirror the divine order of the cosmos.

Even in more modern times, these principles persist. The United States Capitol, the Washington Monument, and the layout of Washington, DC, itself reflect Masonic influences—built on axial alignments, sacred geometric ratios, and symbolic geometry intended to resonate with cosmic archetypes. The city's design encodes pentagrams, vesica piscis shapes, and golden ratio proportions.

In these spaces, even silence hums. Sacred geometry, then, is more than a design language. It is the bridge between consciousness and construction.

Imagine living in a home whose proportions are tuned to the golden ratio—a space where every wall, window, and room is in harmony with the spirals of your DNA and the arcs of the Milky Way.

Not just aesthetically pleasing but biologically calming. A place where your nervous system softens, your breath deepens, and your thoughts begin to organize themselves into clarity—simply because the space is in tune.

Just as we see in cymatics, the more coherent the vibration, the more refined the form. In nature this coherence is everywhere. Life, at its core, is **a song made visible**.

Your body is no exception.

THE CONSCIOUS CYMATIC FIELD: YOU ARE THE FREQUENCY

> *What you think, you become. What you feel, you attract. What you imagine, you create.*
> —BUDDHA

All things—even your thoughts—vibrate.

Your emotions and inner state produce a frequency. That tone is not passive. It organizes matter as well.

Your body is not separate from the CORE field.

It is part of it—a localized expression of the whole.

A resonant instrument vibrating from within the field, shaped by its harmonic code.

Your form follows the CORE blueprint—a vibrational pattern held in the field, guiding the structure of your cells, your rhythms, and even your thoughts.

You are not just in the field.

You are its design, made visible.

A living, breathing cymatic instrument, projecting frequency and responding to it in every moment. From your heartbeat to your brain waves, your entire system hums with rhythmic motion. These vibrations radiate outward, forming what science recognizes as an electromagnetic field—a measurable space around your body that shifts with your thoughts, emotions, and awareness.[5, 6] An aura.

In essence **you are a walking resonance pattern**.

The HeartMath Institute has shown that your heart emits a field measurable several feet beyond the body—one that becomes more **coherent** when you feel elevated emotions like gratitude, love, or peace.[7, 8] This coherence isn't abstract—it influences your brain waves, hormone production, immune system, and even how others around you feel.

Coherence is harmony.

And harmony is the blueprint of life. When your heart and brain are in sync, your personal frequency becomes ordered—like a pure tone in cymatics. This alignment doesn't happen by chance. It's cultivated through forgiveness, self-reflection, and the release of fear and trauma. As the heart stabilizes, so does the field. Your frequency rises, and the pattern it creates becomes elegant, clear, and symmetrical.

When the tone becomes clear, the pattern becomes beautiful.

The higher the frequency, the finer the form.

As we saw in chapter 2, when you break matter down, you don't find solidity—you find space. Atoms are 99.9999% empty, held together by invisible forces. What appears solid is actually a wave of probabilities, shaped by observation.

This is where consciousness enters, collapsing the wave into a moment in time. But what gives that moment its shape?
Movement.
Energy.
Vibration.

Whether through quantum fields or string theory, modern physics agrees: At the deepest level, particles are vibrations in an invisible field. Each form is simply a different frequency. The solid world isn't solid. It's **harmonic**.

Even light, behaving as both wave and particle, responds to the observer. Time, too, stretches and compresses with motion and gravity. These are not fixed realities. They are *emergent*, shaped by something deeper.

In CR that deeper shaping force is **vibration—consciousness in motion**.

What we call reality is not a fixed backdrop. It is a sounding—a dynamic interplay between consciousness and the field it animates. This is why the same space, the same conversation, the same experience can feel entirely different depending on your inner state.

You're not just reacting to reality.

You're generating it.

And the higher your frequency—your coherence, stillness, and clarity—the more refined the pattern becomes around you.

It's like projecting a film onto a screen.

The reel holds the story, but what you see depends on the clarity of the lens.

At lower states of awareness, the lens is clouded—by trauma, rigidity, or unconscious beliefs. The scene appears distorted. But when the lens is clear—refined through presence, forgiveness, or inner coherence—everything sharpens.

The story doesn't change.
Your frequency brings it into focus.

This isn't mystical wishful thinking. It's resonant physics. Just as sound shapes sand into sacred geometry, your consciousness shapes the structure of your life.

This is the physics of *inner alchemy.*

The Vedas—some of humanity's oldest spiritual texts—echoed this truth millennia ago. In their cosmology *Nāda Brahma* means "**sound is God.**" *Creation didn't begin with form or light but with Śabda—the first vibration in stillness.*

Before the elements, before thought, there was tone. And that tone was not emitted—it was *conscious.*

Om, the sacred syllable, wasn't just a chant. It was believed to be the vibrational seed of existence itself.

In this light the CR model doesn't replace the wisdom of the ancients. **It confirms it.**

The moment your awareness selects a frame, the **frequency** of that awareness sculpts its form.

But what is *form?*

Form is not just physical shape.

It is the structure of the moment—what appears, how it feels, what it means, and how it moves.

It's the geometry of your experience.

- The mood in the air
- The posture of a conversation
- The memory that crystallizes
- The emotion that takes root

Form is the **texture** of reality—how space, time, matter, and meaning organize themselves around your attention. And all of it—every curve, every detail, and every echo—**is shaped by the frequency you bring.**

Each moment arises sculpted by the tone of the consciousness that chooses it. This process, where awareness chooses the frame and vibration shapes the form, is not just personal.

It is **cosmic.**
It is the engine behind all creation.

- Awareness collapses the wave, selecting a frame from infinite possibility.
- The form that frame takes depends entirely on the *frequency of the observer.*

Even Nikola Tesla echoed this truth: "If you want to find the secrets of the universe, think in terms of energy, frequency, and vibration."

Energy. Frequency. Vibration.

These aren't side effects of matter. **They are the architects of it.**

Genesis opens with "Let there be light."
But light wasn't the beginning—it was the result.
First came the Word. The Voice. The Vibration.
Consciousness spoke—and matter listened.

This is the metaphysical blueprint beneath all structure.

CR holds that all matter is the shadow of a vibrational act of consciousness. Every atom, every star, and every thought—a note in the unfolding song of being.

This is not evolution by force—it's evolution by frequency.
Not through striving but through tuning.

- A person vibrating in fear will collapse one type of frame— tense, narrow, reactive.
- A person resonating with gratitude collapses another—open, stable, luminous.

Both people live on the same Earth but *not in the same world.* You don't attract what you *want.* **You attract what you're vibrating.**

The field doesn't wait to respond after the fact—**your inner tone shapes the collapse** itself, moment by moment. And here's the key: Each frame you collapse then feeds back into the tone that created it.

A fearful frame reinforces fear. A coherent frame amplifies coherence.

This is a **vibrational feedback loop.**

If you collapse a reality shaped by anger, distrust, or scarcity, you're more likely to feel those things again in the next moment—strengthening the pattern, making it harder to escape.

This is how **low-frequency states become self-reinforcing**, not because the world is against you but because your vibration is selecting, shaping, and confirming your experience.

But the same is true in the other direction.

When you collapse a frame from love, presence, or gratitude, that frame reflects beauty, insight, and meaning, **which lifts your frequency even higher**, creating a loop of expansion and inner alignment.
    In CR this is how you either spiral into contraction or rise into clarity.
    Not by force.
    But by frequency.

And that frequency isn't determined by surface thoughts. It's set by your dominant emotional tone—your coherence, internal harmony, and state of awareness. When you raise your frequency—through stillness, breath, truth, and feeling—you refine your cymatic field. And your outer world responds—people, insights, synchronicities, and opportunities begin to reorganize around your tone.

But as we discussed your cymatic field isn't self-contained. Just as sound interacts with air, your resonance interacts with others. Your personal field doesn't stop at the edge of your skin. It extends outward, **interacting with the fields of others**—merging, repelling, syncing, or distorting based on other frequencies.

Every conversation, every space you enter is a vibrational exchange. Your field is always interacting—shaping and being shaped. You are not isolated in your resonance. You are woven into a shared, sensing matrix. The CORE.

When others enter your field, they don't just notice you—they **entrain** with you. Entrainment is the phenomenon where separate vibrating systems—such as pendulums, fireflies, or even pieces of metal—begin to synchronize their rhythms simply by sharing space. A classic example is when multiple pendulum clocks are mounted on the same wall—over time they begin to swing in perfect unison.[9] Vibrations travel between them until they match and find harmony.

Entrainment is a hidden law of nature: **Rhythm seeks unity**.

You see it everywhere—from heartbeats syncing between lovers[10] to the coordinated flashing of fireflies in a forest. Even menstrual cycles among women living or working in proximity have been observed to synchronize over time—a subtle biological rhythm aligning through shared space and resonance.[11]

Studies in neuroscience have even shown that when people sit together in silence, their heart rhythms and brain waves can begin to sync, especially when emotional connection or empathy is present.[12]

This is why calm people calm rooms.
Why a joyful presence feels magnetic.
Why tension spreads like static.
Your frequency is not private.
It's participatory.
You're not just shaping your own frame.
You're cosounding the collective one—moment by moment.

Even the unfolding of human life reflects this harmonic order. The average length of human gestation—280 days—corresponds almost exactly to ten full lunar cycles. Each moon phase, from waxing crescent to waning, echoes through the womb, guiding the development of form like a cosmic metronome. Ancient cultures did not track pregnancy in weeks—they followed the moon.

This is biological entrainment. Just as the moon's gravity pulls the tides, it pulls the amniotic tides within us. The menstrual cycle mirrors the lunar month, averaging 29.5 days, and conception often aligns with the full or new moon in preindustrial societies. Some researchers have even found that women exposed to natural moonlight without artificial interference tend to ovulate more regularly, suggesting that reproduction itself is attuned to the rhythms of light and darkness.

In this view, gestation is not merely biological—it is also cymatic. A body of water shaped by the moon's invisible frequency, developing not at random but in rhythm. Life begins not in isolation but in resonance with the sky.

Even your words carry vibration.

Ancient cultures understood this. In Egypt, India, Tibet, and Kabbalistic traditions, language wasn't just descriptive—it was creative. Words were spells. Tones were tools. Names were maps of essence.

Our ancestors knew this intuitively: **Vowels were not just sounds— they were forces**. In many languages vowels were considered sacred tones—pure carriers of frequency. Some researchers using high-speed, sound-field imaging have shown that prolonged vowel sounds such as "Ah" or "Om" generate **symmetrical, torus-like pressure fields** in the air—like little sonic doughnuts pulsing vibrations from the mouth.[13]

The word wasn't metaphor. It was energy.

The same applies to space.

Sacred sites, temples, and natural vortices often feel different not because of what's there but because of what's been **sounded** there. Every location, every object, every body is a song in slow motion. This is why some places feel holy, some objects feel charged, and some memories hum with emotion long after they've passed. Vibration doesn't just pass through—it lingers. It imprints.

Emerging research in biofield science shows that water and living tissue can store and respond to vibration, retaining the memory of frequencies long after the sound has passed.[14]

Like sand, water is another medium that takes shape based on frequency.

EXHIBIT 3B

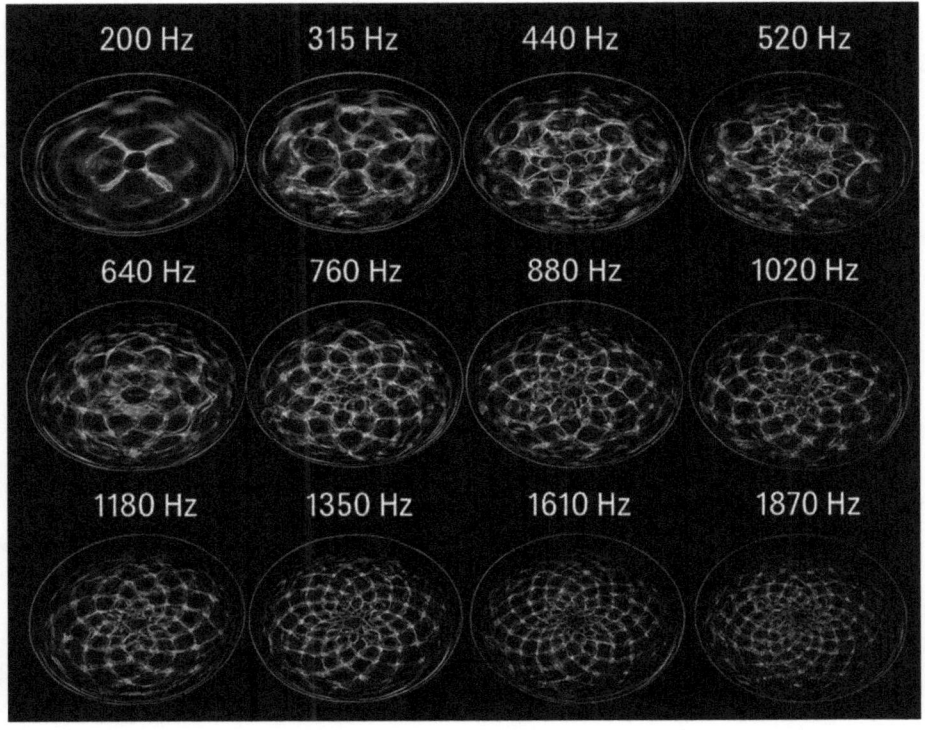

Above: *Illustrative cymatic pattern generated in water using focused vibration. This is what harmony looks like in motion—your body, breath, and words produce similar fields every moment.*

Now consider this: Your body is made up of 70–80% water.

Every word you speak, especially to yourself, is a vibrational instruction to the water within. It shapes the water's structure within yourself. Loving words bring coherence. Angry words bring distortion. When you say, "I'm a failure," your cells feel it. When you whisper, "I'm healing," they listen.

Now think of how this affects a **broadcast system like your DNA**—a spiral antenna of water-bound information, constantly receiving and transmitting frequency. The shape of your words shapes the water. And the water shapes the signal.

This is the foundation of **vibrational medicine**—the use of sound, frequency, and resonance to restore balance in the body and field. Ancient Egypt understood this deeply. Their **sound healing chambers**, such as those at Saqqâra, were constructed with resonant stone architecture designed to amplify specific tones, tuning the human body like an instrument.

In the twentieth century, pioneers such as **Dr. Royal Rife** proposed that every organ[15]—and even every disease—had its own frequency and that healing could occur by targeting imbalances with precise tones. Others, such as **Dr. Peter Guy Manners**,[16] developed vibrational therapy systems based on the idea that healthy tissues resonate at specific frequencies.

From binaural beats to tuning forks, chanting to 432 Hz healing music, practitioners today continue this lineage, using sound to recalibrate the field.

Modern science is beginning to validate what the ancients knew.

- Ultrasound waves are used to break apart kidney stones.[17]
- Pulsed electromagnetic (EMF) fields are applied to promote bone and tissue healing.[18]

- Researchers are now exploring targeted frequencies to destroy cancer cells—without drugs or surgery.[19]

As it turns out, *harmony heals*. Because vibration doesn't just shape form—**it brings it back into harmony**.

You are a resonant system. And language is the tuning fork.

This is why sacred traditions used mantras, chants, and prayers, not just to please the divine but to align the human. Every syllable was an instrument. Every word and vowel, a waveform.

Language is a directed vibration of consciousness, one that *simultaneously selects and sculpts* the moment. The words you choose carry the tone of your vibration, and they shape the frame of the moment that follows.

When your words are coherent, your life begins to echo that tone.

When your words are dissonant, the frame you collapse reflects it—scattered, unstable, unclear.

Think of how different it feels to say "I can't do this" *versus* "I'm figuring it out."

Both may reflect a challenge, but each carries a radically different frequency—one contracts your field; the other expands it. One shuts down potential; the other opens the door to new possibilities.

This is also why words spoken in anger, especially ***curse words***, carry such a distinct charge. To *curse* someone is not just to express frustration; it is to aim those vowels, or little sonic doughnuts we discussed earlier, to inflict harm and send out a frequency that reshapes the water molecules in a person's internal structure.

The term itself reveals the truth: You are quite literally **placing a curse**—you are creating a dissonant tone that shapes the frame of the moment and affects the target's internal structure.

These vibrations don't vanish. They echo—through your body, through your environment, and through the collective field. Angry or hostile language collapses reality into harder, sharper frames—moments filled with tension, defensiveness, and instability. In contrast intentional words spoken with clarity or care become harmonics, tuning your reality and those around you to coherence.

Imagine a waiter who's just been berated by a customer—shouted at, demeaned, humiliated. In that moment it's not just the words that cut—it's the *frequency* behind them. The waiter's internal waters—literal molecules—reorganize under the force of that vibration, shifting into jagged, chaotic patterns. The body tightens. The field distorts. And without realizing it, the waiter **entrains** to that dissonance.

The angry customer's field became dominant, imprinting its rhythm onto the waiter's. Their inner harmony was disrupted by proximity alone.

Moments later another table is seated—polite, kind, maybe even joyful—but the waiter snaps, frowns, or dismisses them coldly.

Why? Because the waiter is still vibrating with the **previous pattern**.
The internal structure has already shifted. The tone has already been set.
And now that frequency spreads—affecting others in the room, reshaping future interactions, and collapsing new frames into tension.

This is how incoherence multiplies.
Not just emotionally but vibrationally.
One dissonant moment becomes a node of resonance—entraining

others, distorting the field, and rippling outward through the collective.

Each interaction doesn't just stay local—it ripples. Your personal field merges briefly with another's, and the CORE field takes note. These exchanges—small gestures, passing words, quiet reactions—become subtle imprints on a much larger canvas.

The CORE field is not static. **It breathes. It shifts. It listens.**

Every vibration you emit contributes to its motion, like a drop in a vast ocean. One moment of fear can tighten the collective rhythm. One act of grace can soften it. This is the **butterfly effect in vibrational form**, where even a whisper of coherence can echo across unseen distances, shaping moments you'll never witness, in lives you'll never meet.

And when one person awakens—when their vibration rises, aligns, and stabilizes—**it is not an isolated event**.
 It is a shift in the field itself.
 A new harmonic introduced into the CORE.

As Emerson once suggested, the Over-Soul connects all things. The awakening of one soul, in truth, is not a personal transformation.

It is a cosmic one.

In the next section, we'll map how these frequencies evolve, showing how rising vibration leads to more intricate, beautiful forms, just as it does in cymatics. Because in truth your spiritual evolution is not abstract.

It is measurable. It is visible.

It is geometric.

PATTERN PROGRESSION: THE FREQUENCY LADDER OF CONSCIOUSNESS

There is geometry in the humming of the strings.
There is music in the spacing of the spheres.
—PYTHAGORAS

In cymatics the lesson is simple yet profound: As frequency increases, so does form.

You are already composed of the building blocks of sacred geometry. The only difference between chaos and coherence in your life is the **frequency of your field**. As your awareness rises—through presence, stillness, clarity, and alignment—so does the frequency of your consciousness. Your internal vibration increases, and the pattern you project becomes more refined.

You don't just see more—you shape more. Reality becomes more refined. Time slows. Meaning deepens. And the outer world begins to echo your inner tone.

Just as sound frequencies shape visible matter in cymatics, your **brain waves** shape your internal world—thoughts, emotions, perception. These waves, measured in hertz, range from the slow delta of deep sleep to the rapid-fire **gamma** associated with peak awareness and unity consciousness.

Brain waves are vibrational in nature—rhythmic pulses moving through your nervous system and beyond. They are the vibrational signature of consciousness itself, broadcasting your inner state into the fabric of reality.

Just as a cymatic plate reveals sound as form, your life reflects mind as pattern. As your brain waves shift into higher frequencies, your cymatic field refines, just like a tone sculpting a more intricate design.

Let's explore how vibration becomes form, not just visually but emotionally and experientially.

EXHIBIT 3C

Frequency (Hz)	Cymatic Pattern	Emotional/ Consciousness State	CR Interpretation
40–100 Hz	Blurred, irregular blobs	Fear, anger, confusion	Fragmented awareness collapsing chaotic frames
200–400 Hz	Basic circular formations	Routine, neutral, mild tension	Low coherence; basic structure with minimal harmony
500–700 Hz	Geometric, symmetrical grids	Calm, centered, thoughtful	Conscious organization; pattern gaining structure
800–1,000 Hz	Complex, layered mandalas	Gratitude, joy, insight	High coherence; projecting harmonic experience
1,000+ Hz	Fractal spirals, radiant symmetry	Love, awe, unity	Stabilized waveform; form aligned with the CORE field

Above: This chart reflects how physical matter responds to increasing acoustic frequencies in cymatics—and serves as a metaphor for how your internal state may shape the external pattern of your life.

This isn't just about sound.

It's about **states of being**.

What appears before you is not chosen by accident—it is sculpted in real time by the tone of awareness selecting it.

This is the quiet truth behind everything we've built in CR so far:

- **Consciousness (awareness itself)** is the *cause* of wave function collapse.
- **The frequency or vibrational quality of that awareness (i.e., brain wave state)** determines the *structure* the collapse resolves into.
- Just as different notes produce different cymatic forms, different states of awareness yield different experiences of reality.

And this is how **reality builds itself around you**:

- Low frequency creates unstable patterns—life feels heavy, scattered, or unclear.
- Higher frequency refines the pattern—life becomes more meaningful, flowing, and aligned.
- At peak coherence your consciousness resonates with the greater CORE field, and reality becomes radiant, fluid, and whole.

CR offers a unifying view: **Consciousness expresses itself through frequency.** And frequency is what organizes form—whether it moves as sound, light, thought, or brain wave. Your inner state is not abstract—it is the architect.

Just as water freezes into different crystals depending on vibrational input, your reality crystallizes into patterns shaped not by effort but by frequency.

You shape the world, from the inside out.
The key is not control but resonance.
Not willpower but frequency.
Raise your awareness.
Tune your field.
And the pattern will follow.

Your heartbeat, your brain waves, your breath—each is a rhythmic pulse. A pattern. A broadcast. These rhythms act like internal cymatic plates, shaping your physiology and perception moment by moment. Just as sand arranges into pattern from sound, your biochemistry and emotion organize around these pulses. This is your resonance signature—the vibrational fingerprint you carry into every room, conversation, and thought.

As you shift your awareness, you alter those vibrational patterns. And as those vibrational patterns change, so does your experience of the world.

This is why elevated states—peace, love, awe—don't just *feel* better. They resonate better. They entrain your body and your surroundings into harmony. In the same way sand arranges into symmetry when touched by the right tone, your life arranges into clarity when shaped by a coherent mind and heart.

The same laws that shape stars, shape you.

And just as we tune an instrument to bring it into harmony, so, too, can we tune ourselves.

In the next section, we'll explore how this **personal tuning** works, how your consciousness acts as a frequency generator, creating the pattern of your experience in real time.

The song of the universe is not distant.
It is already playing—through you.
You are not just an audience to its melody.
You are its instrument.
And as we'll see next, you can tune yourself to sing it well.

RECAP: CHAPTER 3: THE SCULPTOR OF FORM

In this chapter we followed the journey from **observation to vibration** and saw how reality does not merely appear but is **shaped by sound**.

We learned the following:

- **Cymatics** reveals the hidden power of vibration, turning invisible waves into visible form.
- **Sacred geometry** isn't just art—it's the architecture of vibration. Spirals, hexagons, and fractals aren't designed—they emerge, revealing the hidden order of the CORE field wherever frequency stabilizes into form.
- Our **bodies and lives** are cymatic fields—structured by biology, emotion, intention, and frequency.
- **Thoughts, words, and emotions are vibrational forces**, sculpting your field, your health, and your relationships.
- As our **internal frequency rises**, the patterns we project become more refined, harmonious, and radiant, just as higher tones sculpt more intricate cymatic forms.

From the whisper of a mantra to the heartbeat of galaxies, vibration is not a metaphor.

It is the medium of manifestation.

In chapter 4 we'll dive deeper into the **electromagnetic body** and how consciousness tunes reality through the **frequency of the brain**, mapping the field with intention, coherence, and awareness.

4

THE FREQUENCY
OF AWARENESS

*What we are today comes from our thoughts of
yesterday, and our present thoughts build our life of
tomorrow: our life is the creation of our mind.*
—BUDDHA, *DHAMMAPADA* (A FOUNDATIONAL BUDDHIST TEXT OF
MORAL AND PHILOSOPHICAL VERSES ATTRIBUTED TO THE BUDDHA)

THE BRAIN'S FREQUENCY MAP

The ship now hovered in near-Earth orbit, but the true journey had not been through space. It had been inward.

Time hadn't merely passed externally—it had expanded, dilated, even paused, as if obeying some deeper internal law. The crew hadn't stumbled into this shift. They had *crafted* it—*with intention*. They were no longer passive observers of the quantum sea. They had become navigators of the invisible, steering not with instruments but with **consciousness**. They weren't reacting to space-time—they were **tuning it**, aligning their consciousness like musicians adjusting pitch, guiding the spaceship not by propulsion but by frequency. Between Saturn and Earth, they had practiced.

Eyes closed. Breath slowed. Attention sharpened.

They had begun to shift internal gears, moving deliberately between states of awareness, like sliding through octaves of thought and presence. It wasn't guesswork. It was self-reflection.

And it began in the brain.

Back on Earth, scientists call it **electroencephalography (EEG)**—a technology that lets us measure the rhythmic electrical activity of the brain, recorded through sensors placed on the scalp. What looks like simple waves on a screen are the signature pulses of awareness itself.

These waves—measured in hertz (Hz)—form distinct bands, each corresponding to a different **state of consciousness**. They are not random fluctuations. They are structured, layered, harmonic. Like a symphony unfolding in the skull.

These are the major **brain wave frequencies**:

- **Delta (0.5–4 Hz):** The slowest waves, tied to deep, dreamless sleep. A realm of pure restoration. In this state consciousness fades into the background, yet the body heals, and the spirit may drift far.
- **Theta (4–8 Hz):** The zone of twilight. Daydreams, trance, the edge of sleep. A creative threshold where imagery and memory rise like mist.
- **Alpha (8–12 Hz):** Calm, reflective wakefulness. The brain in neutral gear—receptive, open, peaceful. Often accessed through meditation or relaxed attention.

- **Beta (12–30 Hz):** The domain of alert thinking, focus, problem-solving. Here, the mind is active, linear, and often locked into the rhythm of external demands.
- **Gamma (30–100+ Hz):** The summit. Rapid, synchronized bursts that appear during moments of profound insight, heightened awareness, and mystical unity. These waves ripple like lightning across the entire brain, binding perception into a singular clarity. Gamma is not just clarity—it's temporal depth. More presence, more time.

Each of these waves is like a **station on the dial of awareness**. The brain is never fixed on just one, but one will usually dominate. Shift the dial, and reality itself begins to shift.

This brings us to an important thread carried forward from chapter 3: If sound can organize the physical world into geometry, can the brain's electrical rhythm create a vibration that organizes our world in the same way?

BRIDGING CYMATICS AND BRAIN WAVES: THE HIDDEN HARMONY BETWEEN SOUND AND THOUGHT

Brain waves do not merely reflect consciousness. They shape its expression.

While brain waves are measured in low-frequency electrical activity, ranging from 0.5 to 100 Hz, they share an astonishing parallel with much higher frequencies explored in chapter 3, where sound creates form through cymatics. At first glance these two frequency domains may seem unrelated: One is the soft electrical hum of your neurons; the other is audible vibration (sound) moving through air, water, or sand. But they are deeply linked. They both follow the same rule: Frequency creates form.

In cymatic experiments we saw how tones between hundreds and thousands of hertz could sculpt matter into geometric patterns—grids, mandalas, spirals. Raise the frequency, and the form becomes more complex and ordered. Lower it, and the pattern becomes crude and chaotic.

Now think of your brain. It also runs on waves. These frequencies are lower than cymatic tones, but they do something similar: They turn scattered thoughts into a clear, unified experience. In cymatics it's visible form. In the brain it's lived experience. Both are governed by the same principle—vibration arranges chaos into pattern.

EXHIBIT 4A

Aspect	Cymatic Frequencies	Brain Wave Frequencies
Typical Range	100 Hz–10,000+ Hz (audible + ultrasonic)	0.5 Hz–100 Hz
Output	Visible geometry and spatial structure	Conscious perception, attention, time experience

- Sound must move **through space** and **physical medium** like air or water. To generate visible structure, it needs faster Hz.
- Brain waves don't need to travel in space—they operate **electromagnetically**, transmitting meaning across neurons via **resonant fields**. Their signal is slower in hertz but more **efficient per cycle** because it encodes **perceptual information, coherence, and awareness**.

How are sound and brain waves connected?

The connection lies not in their numerical frequency but in their **function: using vibration to organize structure and experience.**

A disordered beta state—characterized by high beta spiking and lack of coherence—often correlates with stress or fragmentation. While beta enables focus and problem-solving, its dysregulation produces noise, not clarity. A higher-frequency state, such as coherent gamma, generates clarity, integration, and a refined sense of time and self. So instead of shaping sand, your brain waves shape how you feel, what you notice, and how you remember. They give form to your inner world—like cymatics shaping water into pattern, your thoughts shape awareness into meaning.

The **brain's frequency is the** *internal cymatic engine* shaping our lived experience.

In the same way, your brain's subtle frequencies and cymatic sound vibrations are two expressions of the same principle: Vibration shapes structure. Think of your consciousness as a musician playing two instruments at once—one tuned to sculpt the world around you; the other tuned to shape the world within. Your thoughts and your voice work the same way—one shapes your *inner* state; the other shapes the world around you. Sound shapes the world. Brain waves shape the self.

EXHIBIT 4B

The sound frequency you emit
shapes your external environment.

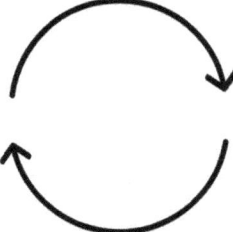

The brain frequency you embody
shapes your internal experience.

The brain frequency you live in shapes how you feel inside, and that feeling becomes the tone you send out. Whether through your voice, posture, or presence, your vibration changes the space around you. The world responds not to your thoughts but to your signal. And what comes back becomes the next moment you experience. The field responds not to your intention but to your vibration. That response becomes part of what you observe, closing the loop between inner state and outer feedback.

And the field's response doesn't just complete the loop—it becomes the next prompt for your awareness. The observer returns, now shaped by its own creation. Each moment it perceives alters the field, and each alteration bends back upon the perceiver. In witnessing reality it is redefined by it. Your awareness is not a neutral spectator—it is an evolving node in a feedback loop of becoming. The vibration you emit sculpts the next frame, and the frame you receive reshapes the lens through which you look. Like a musician hearing the echo of their own note, the observer is transformed by the very song it sets in motion—entering again with new tone, new shape, new self.

But they are two layers of the same instrument.

In this way chapters 3 and 4 form a harmonic pair. Chapter 3 showed how vibration sculpts the visible world through sound. Chapter 4 now reveals how vibration sculpts awareness through the brain. Cymatics gives us a map of how **outer matter is tuned**. EEG gives us a map of how **inner reality is tuned**.

Together they point to a unified truth: Whether it's grains of sand forming mandalas or moments of life forming meaning, **vibration is the architect. Frequency is the brush. And consciousness is the hand that holds it.**

EXHIBIT 4C

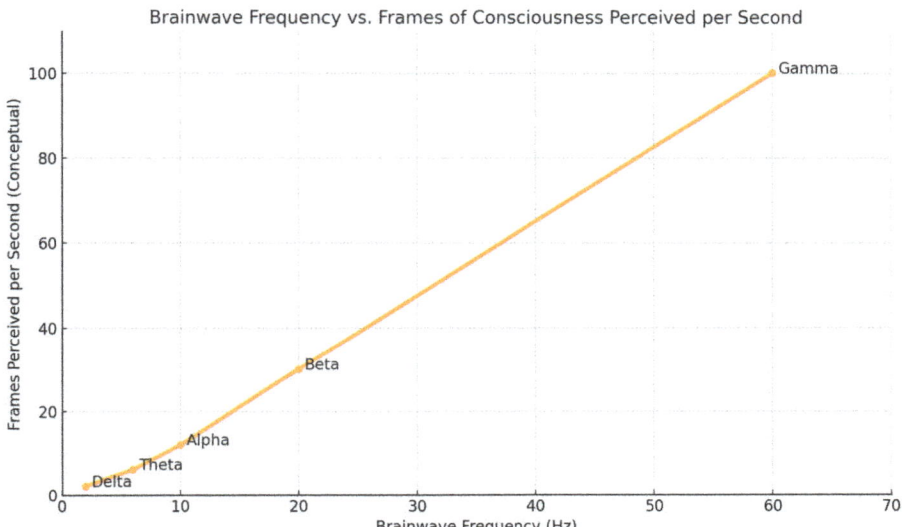

Above: As brain wave frequency rises, the depth of conscious entry into each frame increases. "Frames per second" here symbolizes the richness and resolution of each experienced moment, not how many images are processed but how completely awareness inhabits each one. In gamma time may feel slower, but experience becomes profoundly fuller.

This does not mean simply processing more frames in a shorter time span, such as by watching a video at 1.5 × speed. It means entering each perceptual "frame" with greater awareness—extracting more detail, meaning, and emotional texture from each moment. Higher-frequency brain waves (such as gamma) do not make time faster—they make each moment thicker, more layered, more luminous.

At low frequencies perception skips across the surface of reality—like glancing at pages without reading them. At high frequencies time slows down internally and sinks into the moment—like reading a page so deeply it comes alive.

YOU ARE THE NAVIGATOR: CONSCIOUSNESS AS A VEHICLE THROUGH TIME

But this influence goes deeper than neurobiology.

In the CR model, you are not merely experiencing frames—you are traveling through them.

Each shift in frequency is not just a change in perception—it's a change in trajectory.

This is more than a metaphor. CR suggests your brain is not just processing reality—it's tuning it. Like a dial, it selects which version of reality you step into. Your awareness doesn't just color perception—it steers it. You are the navigator, not by propulsion but by precision.

You are not anchored to a single timeline or reality. You are a conscious traveler, selecting and sculpting your path through the quantum sea. Just like a photon exists in many states until observed, your consciousness holds many routes, varying timelines and diverging possibilities, until a frame is chosen. That collapse isn't passive. It's a choice.

And when you raise your awareness—through stillness, intention, coherence—you don't just see more. You *move* differently.

- A scattered mind flickers between frames unconsciously, reacting to noise.
- A coherent mind locks into a steady rhythm—like surfing a current of chosen moments.

But the implications ripple outward.

Because in the entangled universe, your navigation doesn't happen in isolation. You are not surfing a private stream of reality—you are tuning into a field shared by others. Just as entangled particles reflect each other across vast distances, so, too, does consciousness: Your state of awareness shapes the field, and the field responds in kind.

Each frame you collapse becomes a signal—one that influences what others perceive, feel, or even choose. The more coherent your vibration, the more harmonically you resonate with the shared field of entangled observers.

So awareness does more than select a timeline.
It synchronizes timelines.
It draws others into coherence.
It pulls potentialities into alignment, not just for you but through you.

This is why the state of your awareness—your vibration, frequency, and clarity—acts like a navigation system.
It doesn't just shape how much you see.
It shapes where you go—across time, across possibility.

The ancient mystics were right: "You reap what you sow."

In CR terms: As you vibrate, so you create.

You are not a solitary observer drifting through possibility. You are a tuning fork in the quantum symphony—selecting the music, guiding the tempo, drawing others into harmony.

You feel it all the time.

- When you're focused, reality sharpens. Beta dominates.
- When you meditate, the world softens. Alpha opens the door.
- In deep sleep you vanish from the world entirely. Delta carries you away.
- And in rare, electrifying moments—of love, revelation, or awe—gamma sings.

Let's recap.

As we learned in **chapter 1**, Einstein showed us that time bends with motion; CR expanded this by showing that time also bends with **awareness**.

In **chapter 2** we discovered that **consciousness affects matter**, selecting from a wave of possibilities and writing reality into being. Time isn't flowing past you—it's being drawn into form by your attention. The observer doesn't just see the moment—it **chooses it**.

In **chapter 3** we added that once a frame is chosen, it is shaped by **vibration**. Just as sound sculpts sand into mandalas, your inner frequency—emotional tone, coherence, presence—shapes the **texture** of each moment. By texture, we mean the felt quality of the moment—its emotional granularity, depth of tone, and narrative richness. A coarse texture feels rushed or reactive; a refined texture feels coherent, meaningful, and full. Higher vibration produces **finer, more meaningful forms**.

Now in **chapter 4** we see that the **resolution** of each moment depends on your **brain wave frequency**. Resolution refers to the clarity and perceptual detail your awareness brings into each frame—like shifting from a blurry to a high-definition photo. Higher brain wave frequencies allow you to process and absorb more within a single moment. It's not just seeing more—it's seeing more clearly. Your awareness doesn't just choose the frame and shape it—it determines **how clearly you experience it**. Faster brain waves don't rush time—they deepen it. In gamma you **enter each frame more fully**. The result is not speed but richness.

This is why time seems to **slow during awe, crisis, or deep presence**. Not because time has changed but because you have. You have dilated time not by spaceship but by consciousness. You are collapsing richer reality into each moment—high-frequency awareness processing more slices of now with precision, clarity, and depth.

To further clarify how this all fits together, let's revisit the full creative process of consciousness.

- **Step 1:** You Choose the Frame (Chapter 2)—Just like a film director selects a shot, your awareness chooses a moment from the infinite stream of possibility.
    - When you're anxious or distracted, you collapse frames, reactively flipping through reality like someone channel surfing without paying attention.
    - When you're focused and present, you select frames with intention—like a photographer waiting for perfect light, choosing not just what's next but what matters.
    - *You are the one collapsing the moment into being.*

- **Step 2:** You Shape the Frame with Vibration (Chapter 3)—Once you've selected the moment, your inner frequency gives it texture and tone—just like a cymatic vibration shapes a pattern in sand or water.
    - If your internal state is chaotic or fearful, the frame becomes jagged, incoherent.
    - If your state is loving, calm, or grateful, that same moment crystallizes into beauty, symmetry, and depth.
    - *Your vibration determines what the frame becomes.*

- **Step 3:** You Control the Resolution of the Frame (Chapter 4)—Your brain wave sets the "frame rate" of your consciousness—like adjusting how many stills your camera captures per second. The faster the brain wave, the more frames you stitch into each moment—and the deeper your experience becomes. Your brain's frequency sets the clarity and richness of what you experience.

- Low frequencies (theta and delta) are like blurry photos. They're important for dreaming and restoration but not great for clear perception.
- High frequencies (especially gamma) are like shooting in 4k, ultra-HD. You see into each frame with greater detail.
- *Gamma awareness is like stepping into a slow-motion, high-definition version of reality, where everything becomes luminous, layered, and alive.*

While these are presented as steps, they all happen simultaneously.

The frame is chosen, shaped, and resolved in a single act of awareness—like a musician striking one note that instantly carries tone, timing, and texture. You don't collapse reality in stages. You do it all at once—with each breath, each glance, each thought. Conscious creation isn't a sequence—it's a synthesis.

In this view awareness isn't just a flashlight. It's a composer—tuning frequency, selecting frames, conducting time. Change your brain wave, refine your tone, and your world reorients around you.

To see how this plays out in real life, let's walk through a moment we've all experienced—a simple human interaction that contains the full arc of conscious creation.

Let's say you're sitting across from your partner at the end of a long day.

You're both tired. You've barely spoken all evening. There's a pause, and then they say something sharp. Maybe it's criticism. Maybe it touches a wound.

FRAME SELECTION (CHAPTER 2)

In that instant your awareness chooses a frame to collapse.

- You could react defensively, choosing a frame of conflict.
- Or you could pause, take a breath, and choose a frame of inquiry or compassion.

Unconscious choice (low awareness): You snap back. The moment becomes one of escalation.

Conscious choice (high awareness): You soften. You ask, "What's really going on?" The moment becomes connection.

You chose the frame. You're not just in the moment—you chose which version of the moment came into being.

VIBRATIONAL SHAPING (CHAPTER 3)

Now that the frame has collapsed, your inner vibration starts shaping its texture.

- If you're carrying resentment or stress, your energy distorts the moment—it feels harsh, closed, jagged.
- If you're rooted in calmness or love, the vibration smooths the edges. Even if the words are hard, the feeling of the moment becomes one of safety and healing.

You shaped the frame with your vibration. Just like a cymatic plate, your body translated emotion into structure. The tone you carry gives the moment its texture.

RESOLUTION AND CLARITY (CHAPTER 4)

Your brain wave state determines how much of the moment you actually see.

- If you're in beta (tense, scattered), your perception narrows. You miss the subtle cues—the flicker in their eye, the hesitancy in their voice. Maybe you black out, not remembering your actions or after a few days cannot even recall the argument or what caused it.
- But if you're in gamma—even briefly—you catch it all. The microexpressions. The truth beneath their words. Time slows. You become fully present.

You experienced the moment through a chosen level of clarity. It wasn't just what happened—it was what you noticed, what you allowed, and what became real.

This is the full arc of conscious creation—selection, shaping, perception, and response. In every moment your awareness is collapsing reality into form, your vibration is tuning its quality, and your brain is setting the clarity of the frame. You're not reacting to life. You're composing it.

In sum:

Chapter 2 describes how we select reality (choose the frame).

Chapter 3 reveals how your vibration sculpts it.

Chapter 4 shows you how clearly you can experience or perceive it and the relative feeling of time.

So while **time may appear fixed from the outside**, your **inner frequency is the true clock.**

So we now ask a profound question: **Is time measured by the ticking of a clock or by the depth of your experience within it?**

One hour spent in distraction might blur into nothing. One hour in awe, heartbreak, or insight can echo for a lifetime.

Then what matters most isn't how long a moment lasts as measured by a clock *but how fully you experience it.*

This happens when the entire brain locks into harmony—when the frequency peaks, the pattern stabilizes, and the observer tunes fully into the CORE field.

That's the gateway to gamma.

And that clarity when in gamma—the resolution of your awareness—may be the deepest form of power.

GAMMA: THE PEAK OF INTEGRATION
There is a moment when thought dissolves into knowing.
When the world feels not separate but unified.
When time doesn't pass—you enter it.
This is gamma.

In the spectrum of brain wave activity, gamma is the highest known frequency, typically measured from 40 Hz and above, sometimes exceeding 100 Hz in rare, advanced states. It's fast, yes, but not frantic. Gamma is not the jitter of anxiety or the noise of overthinking. It's the pulse of pure coherence.

At the gamma level, the brain isn't just active—it's synchronized. Different regions fire in harmony across vast distances. Sensory input, memory, emotion, and insight become one fluid stream of awareness.

GAMMA AND THE AWAKENING MIND
Researchers first began to glimpse the mystery of gamma when studying Tibetan monks in deep meditation. Equipped with EEG caps, these lifelong practitioners showed bursts of gamma activity far

beyond anything seen in the general population, especially during practices of compassion, deep stillness, or transcendence.[1]

In one study monks producing sustained 80–100 Hz activity described experiences of timelessness, boundless love, and unity with all life.[2]

This wasn't mild relaxation. It was total integration—a state of being where awareness was luminous, steady, and unbroken.

Gamma and Downloads

Many spiritual seekers describe receiving "downloads"—sudden bursts of insight or entire packets of understanding that arrive not as thoughts but as fully formed ideas. Words come after. The experience itself is wordless.

Gamma appears to be the neurological signature of these states.

You don't figure something out.

It lands, whole and immediate, like a frame you didn't collapse but emerged from the CORE field directly.

This experience isn't limited to mystics. Many of history's greatest minds have described similar phenomena.

- **Nikola Tesla**, inventor and visionary behind alternating current (the system that powers modern electricity), the induction motor, wireless transmission, and even the foundations of modern radio, described receiving entire inventions as fully formed visions. He once said, "My brain is only a receiver. In the Universe, there is a core from which we obtain knowledge, strength and inspiration."

Tesla often described entire machines arriving in his mind spontaneously, complete with blueprints, dimensions, and mechanical function.

He would rotate them mentally, test them in his imagination, and refine them—all without writing a single line or building a prototype.

- **Srinivasa Ramanujan**, the Indian mathematical prodigy, claimed his extraordinary equations came to him in dreams and visions. He said they were "divinely revealed" by the goddess Namagiri. Many of his results—initially dismissed—later proved groundbreaking in number theory, string theory, and even black hole entropy.
- **Dmitri Mendeleev**, creator of the periodic table, recounted that the layout of elements came to him in a dream—perfectly ordered and complete.
- **August Kekulé**, a German chemist, discovered the ring structure of benzene after seeing a vision of a snake biting its tail—a symbol of wholeness—while slipping into a dreamlike trance on a bus.
- **Carl Jung** and **Wolfgang Pauli**, pioneers of psychology and quantum physics, respectively, both explored a phenomenon they called *synchronicity*—a connecting principle suggesting that the mind can access meaning beyond linear cause and effect.

These weren't slow, deductive discoveries. They were flashes of entire frameworks, delivered as if from a deeper intelligence.

CR proposes that such downloads arise when the brain enters sustained **gamma coherence**, unlocking a field of insight beyond ordinary awareness. The result isn't just brilliance. It's integration—knowledge arriving as wholeness, bypassing logic, and emerging as resonance.

In these states you don't generate ideas.

You tune into them.

In CR terms gamma may represent a momentary merger between the observer and the unifying CORE field we discussed in chapter 2—a glimpse of source awareness where observer, vibration, and structure are no longer separate steps but a singular act of being.

GAMMA AND BRAIN COHERENCE

Unlike lower states, where brain regions operate semi-independently, firing out of sync like instruments warming up before a concert, gamma unifies the network. The prefrontal cortex (thinking), visual cortex (seeing), limbic system (feeling), and deeper thalamic regions (sensory relay) pulse in lockstep.

It's like an orchestra that usually plays in scattered sections—strings here, percussion there, each absorbed in its own rhythm. But in gamma every instrument locks into the same tempo. The CORE field becomes the orchestra's conductor.

The result is not more noise—it's a symphony.

And this is what makes gamma so rare—and so powerful.

Most people never reach gamma in daily life, not because they can't but because the conditions are seldom met. Our normal waking states, especially beta, are often chaotic.

- Thought loops
- Stress reactions
- Distraction by devices and demands

Like musicians each playing a different song, the brain becomes fragmented—still functioning but noisy and disharmonized. Even alpha and theta states, though more relaxed, rarely achieve the global synchronization needed for gamma.

Gamma, by contrast, is a luminous state of total coherence.

It requires the following:

- **Relaxed but engaged**—The body is at ease, grounded and calm, yet fully present, not drifting toward sleep or dullness.
- **Focused but effortless**—The mind is sharp and alert but without strain or grasping—like being in flow, not in fight.
- **Open but unified**—Awareness is expansive and receptive but not scattered. All parts of you are tuned to the same signal.

TIME, COLLAPSED DIFFERENTLY

In gamma, time behaves strangely.

Moments don't speed by—they deepen. Each frame grows denser, more vivid, more alive with meaning. Gamma doesn't just increase what you process—it expands how fully you *enter* the moment: richly, consciously, and completely.

This may explain the "eternity" reported in mystical states, near-death experiences, or deep meditation, where minutes feel infinite yet grounded in a single, unwavering moment.

In these states time is no longer a **line** you follow. It becomes a **well** you fall into. Gamma offers access to time **not as motion** but as **dimensionality**—a spiral of stillness where the moment widens, and perception sinks deeper into the now.

This mirrors the paradox we explored in chapter 1.

In Einstein's relativity, time slows for an object traveling near the speed of light, not because clocks change but because that object begins to experience **more space-time** within each passing second.

From Earth's perspective the traveler stretches time.
But from the traveler's view, the moment expands.

Likewise, in gamma, awareness doesn't flit across more frames—**it enters the still frame**. The mind doesn't race—it **finds coherence**.

Just as a ship nearing light speed experiences one thousand years of Earth time in a single onboard hour, a mind in gamma can experience a thousand lifetimes within a single hour of presence.

In both cases the principle is the same: **more awareness per frame = more time inside each moment.**

Gamma achieves what relativity does externally but from the inside out.

It is **inner time dilation**, not via motion but via integration.

Einstein showed us that time is flexible, contingent on the observer's velocity. CR builds on this by showing that time is equally flexible based on the observer's **frequency**. Velocity bends space-time, but **vibration** bends experience. Gamma is the harmonic proof of that. It's the state where consciousness transcends linear time, not by escaping it but by deepening it.

In CR this makes gamma not just a peak state but a **portal**—a threshold where presence becomes architecture, and time ceases to flow because you've stepped inside it.

GAMMA AS THE THRESHOLD

In the CR model, gamma is more than a high-performance brain state.

It's a threshold state, where the mind's signal becomes so clear, so resonant that it can interact directly with deeper fields of reality.

It's not the end of awareness—it's the threshold where awareness merges with the CORE field.

There is growing evidence—both scientific and spiritual—that gamma isn't just a peak state; it may be our original state.

A new kind of participation in the structure of time, form, and meaning.

When the brain enters sustained gamma, something profound happens.
    It synchronizes.

Multiple regions—across emotion, vision, memory, and cognition—fire together in a seamless rhythm.
    Not randomly. Not reactively. But coherently.

It's like a great machine finally operating at full capacity.
Gears once spinning out of sync begin to align.
Lights across the dashboard blink in harmony.
The system, once noisy and compartmentalized, becomes unified.

Imagine you own a sports car—designed to handle speed, glide through curves, and awaken every sense behind the wheel.

But every day you crawl through city traffic—stop and go, idle, first gear only.
    The engine hums but never roars.
    The machine functions but never fulfills its purpose.
    Then one day you go on vacation and take the car on a highway, finding an open stretch of road.
    You press the pedal gently, then harder.
    Suddenly, the car comes alive.
    Every cylinder fires in harmony.
    The electronic components come alive.
    The entire engine is operating in unison.
    The system that once felt muted now sings.
    The machine is doing what it was built to do.

That's what happens in gamma.

The brain, so often stuck in traffic—disjointed, reactive, compartmentalized—finally finds the open road. Regions that normally fire in isolation begin to synchronize. Emotion, vision, memory, and thought align in a unified rhythm.

This is not a superhuman achievement but rather our *intended state*. It's what the brain was designed to do.

There is emerging evidence that our ancestors didn't just glimpse gamma—they lived closer to it.

Studies of seasoned meditators, indigenous shamans, and contemplatives in deep trance or prayer show sustained bursts of high-frequency gamma far beyond what's typical in the modern brain.[3, 4, 5] Brain scans of Tibetan monks and Yogic adepts reveal a brain that is not fragmented by noise but humming in synchrony.[6] In preliterate societies, where presence was survival, where ritual and rhythm governed life, not clocks and screens, their nervous systems were likely tuned for coherence, not distraction.

Their environment demanded stillness, awareness, integration.

Their brains, in turn, reflected it.

In mythic terms this shift recalls an ancient fall, not from grace but from coherence. A descent not merely into sin but into separation. As modern life fractured our rhythms, so, too, it fractured the mind.

And with that fracture, the music dimmed.

What if Eden wasn't only a place we lost but also a state of resonance we forgot?

Today's divided perception—fragmented, distracted, reactive—may be the symptom of a mind running below its design frequency.

From this perspective gamma isn't something to attain—it's something to remember.

A resonant state where the brain, body, and field become one instrument.
    A tuning to truth.

And yet even gamma may not be the final octave.

Emerging research and rare case studies point to brain wave frequencies above 100 Hz, sometimes reaching 200–600 Hz or more. These are sometimes referred to as lambda waves—the ultrahigh-frequency bursts associated with the most profound states of mystical unity, timeless awareness, and nondual consciousness.

Unlike gamma, which binds the brain into harmony across vast neural networks, lambda appears when the mind itself dissolves, when the "self" merges with the field so completely that even thought, time, and observer fade.

Descriptions from these states—often reported during deep ayahuasca ceremonies, DMT journeys, near-death experiences, or advanced meditative absorption (samadhi)—match this wave band with uncanny precision:

- Complete ego dissolution
- Perception of "other-dimensional" beings or intelligences
- Entry into timeless, formless awareness
- A felt experience of pure light, geometry, or the "source code" of reality

Could lambda represent contact with the first layers of higher-dimensional consciousness?

These realms are normally hidden behind the filter of beta noise and ego structure. In this state awareness doesn't just unify the brain. It unifies with the CORE field itself.

Where gamma is the threshold, lambda may be the crossing over point.

Few reach it. Fewer still return with language to describe the experience. But its existence confirms the deepest message of this chapter:

> *Your consciousness is not confined to the brain.*
> *It is a frequency-tuned field, with higher realms still to be remembered.*

In CR terms gamma and lambda may be the original language of the observer—before fear.
Before fragmentation.
Before forgetting.
A state not lost but *remembered.*
Home.

NEUROCHEMISTRY OF AWARENESS
If frequency is the signal of consciousness, neurochemistry is the tuner.

Your brain is not just a receiver of awareness—it's a dynamic, living instrument constantly shifting what you can perceive. And its key modulators are chemicals—tiny molecular messengers that either open the gates of higher awareness or slam them shut.

CHEMICALS AS FREQUENCY MODULATORS
Neurotransmitters and hormones such as serotonin, dopamine, norepinephrine, cortisol, and even DMT shape the range of brain wave frequencies your mind can access.

These neurotransmitters don't contain meaning or memory themselves.

They're like brightening or dimmer switches. They decide how much of reality your brain can tune into.

They don't create consciousness.
But they govern the clarity and elevation of the state you're in.

Serotonin increases calm receptivity, promoting alpha waves and gentle presence.

Dopamine, linked to pleasure and reward, opens the door to flow states and beta-gamma transitions.

Cortisol and adrenaline, on the other hand, block access to higher frequencies, pulling you down into survival-mode beta or even freezing you in theta panic.

- Brain waves define the frame rate of consciousness.
- Chemicals determine whether you can tune into those frames at all.

HOW STRESS DISRUPTS FREQUENCY

EXHIBIT 4D

Hormone	Function	Brain Wave Frequency Effect
Cortisol	Long-term stress management	Suppresses alpha and gamma; locks into low beta
Adrenaline	Fight-or-flight response	Narrows focus, blocks access to higher cognition
Norepinephrine	Hyperalert scanning	Can spike or crash gamma; increases anxiety/fragmentation

These chemicals don't directly collapse time, but they narrow your brain's ability to perceive frames.

Just like a spider weaves its world through the rhythm of its nervous system, you weave reality through the rhythm of your awareness.

In a famous NASA study,[7] spiders given different drugs spun drastically altered webs—caffeine led to chaos, marijuana to disjointed structure, amphetamines to rushed incompletion. When sober, the web returned to balance and form.

Your consciousness is no different. The coherence of your field determines the structure of your world.

In survival your brain simplifies.

TIME PERCEPTION IS A FUNCTION OF FREQUENCY

EXHIBIT 4E

Brain Wave	Frequency Range	Time Perception Description
Delta/Theta	0.5–8 Hz	Dreamlike, fragmented, dissociative
Alpha	8–12 Hz	Calm, centered, mild expansion
Beta	13–30 Hz	Functional but narrow, linear
Gamma	30–100+ Hz	Timeless, unified, hyperpresent

It is the brain wave frequency that expands time, not the chemical.

But chemicals act as filters, keys, or locks to those frequencies.

Flow states arise when stress hormones are low, dopamine is elevated, and brain wave coherence is high, often entering the beta-gamma threshold. In this state time seems to slow down, effort dissolves, and the sense of "self" as a separate observer fades. You're not doing something—you are it.

Here are some examples of flow:

A surfer gliding down the face of a wave, so attuned that every movement unfolds without thought.

A writer in deep creative focus, losing all awareness of time as paragraphs pour forth in a single stream.

A jazz musician improvising, not planning the notes, just being the music.

In each case beta provides precision, gamma offers coherence, and dopamine floods the system with reward, reinforcing full presence.

Now consider psychedelics such as psilocybin, lysergic acid diethylamide (LSD), or DMT. These compounds alter the neurochemical landscape profoundly.

Thalamic gating is loosened, letting in sensory data that is normally filtered out.

Default mode network activity—linked to ego and mental chatter—is quieted.

Gamma synchrony spikes across regions not usually connected in waking states.

This doesn't create "hallucination" in the typical sense—it reveals what lies behind the veil of filtered perception.

Described effects include the following:

- Timelessness—Minutes feel infinite; moments feel eternal.
- Wordlessness—A felt sense beyond language.
- Unity—The boundary between self and world dissolves.
- Vibrational Saturation—A sense that everything is made of energy, pulsing with aliveness.

These states show us what awareness looks like when the chemical locks are lifted, when frequency is allowed to rise unimpeded. You are not adding something new. You are removing what was blocking access.

But among these medicines, **ayahuasca** deserves special mention.

Unlike other psychedelics, ayahuasca combines **DMT** with mono-amine oxidase (**MAO) inhibitors**, allowing the experience to unfold over hours rather than minutes. What unfolds is not just vision but often **purge**. Vomiting, sweating, shaking, crying, laughing—each a release.

To the outsider it may seem violent, but to the experiencer it is sacred.

What if the purge isn't side effect but signal? What if it is the **body's response to realignment** with the CORE field?

Imagine a ship veering off course for years, then suddenly correcting trajectory. It would shake. It would groan. It would release pressure.

Or think of Neo in *The Matrix*.

When he takes the red pill—the pill of **truth**—he doesn't awaken gently.

He convulses. His body **rejects the illusion** it had mistaken for reality. He vomits.

The purge is not a malfunction.

It is a **necessary recalibration**—a cleansing of false signals so the real signal can come through.

Ayahuasca may do the same.

CR suggests this purging is not random. It is **somatic recalibration**—the clearing of interference, stored trauma, and emotional static so that the CORE frequency can flow through again.

- The visions are not decoration—they are recalibration.
- The purge is not expulsion—it is resonance correction.
- The experience is not escape—it is a **return**.

A return to gamma harmony.
A return to coherence.
A return to the state the system was built to inhabit.

But even gamma may not be the final note. In rare cases—especially in deep ayahuasca states, extended DMT immersion, or advanced meditative absorption—brain wave activity has been observed to surge into an even higher range: lambda, exceeding 200 Hz and reaching up to 600 Hz in some accounts.

This isn't just increased coherence—it's dissolution. At these ultra-high frequencies, the self doesn't simply align with reality; it disappears into it. Identity drops. Time vanishes. The observer dissolves into the observed.

CR suggests this may be the neural signature of total field merger, where consciousness is no longer localized but becomes indistinguishable from the CORE itself.

Where gamma is the orchestra tuned, lambda is the music itself—resonating through no separate player, no separate instrument, just the pure tone of being.

In this light, ayahuasca is not just a psychedelic. It is a **resonance medicine**—a tuner that shakes loose the static and invites the whole self back into alignment.

Like motion sickness from shifting realities too quickly, the purge may be a side effect of reentry, **not into hallucination but into truth**.

And for a time, the veil is lifted.

Let's summarize this clearly.

1. Chemicals modulate your ability to access frequencies. Your inner chemistry is the gatekeeper. Just like fog on a lens, stress hormones blur perception. Love, calm, or psychedelics polish the lens, revealing more.
2. Frequencies determine how many frames you can perceive. A higher brain wave frequency means more slices of reality are stitched together per moment. Gamma = high frame rate = deeper presence.

Fear compresses time.

- You're stuck in low beta (low-frequency awareness). The world feels fast, jagged, reactive. You're not absorbing, just surviving. Like scrolling endlessly through social media: time vanishes but nothing lands. You're flicking through frames without depth, caught in low-resolution mode.

Love expands time.

- Elevated frequency opens perception. You notice the curve of a smile and the warmth of silence. *A long hug that feels like forever, even though only seconds passed.*

Presence feels eternal.

- High frequency + gamma coherence collapses the illusion of linear time. You're fully here. *A deep meditation or awe-inspiring view where you feel no urge to measure time at all.*

THE RETURN PATH

CR does not view stress or fragmentation as moral failings but as frequency states that can be retrained, rebalanced, and rewired.

The way forward is not through willpower alone.

It is through the following:

- Breath
- Practice
- Nutrition
- Stillness
- Compassion
- Joy
- Wisdom
- Knowledge
- Empathy
- Forgiveness
- Love

Each of these modulates your chemistry.
And through that chemistry, you retune your brain.

To bring it full circle, stress is not just emotional—it is **vibrational interference**.

It lowers your frequency by disrupting the chemical environment required for gamma coherence. This, in turn, collapses your ability to perceive frames fluidly.

- In fear time feels fast and jagged because your brain is skipping frames.
- In presence time expands because your frequency is elevated and integrated.

This is why meditation, breathwork, and forgiveness aren't just spiritual ideas. They *biochemically* lift your access to clarity.

RECAP: CHAPTER 4: AWARENESS AS RESOLUTION

If chapter 2 showed us that we choose the frame and chapter 3 showed us that we shape it with vibration to give it texture, then chapter 4 revealed how clearly we can experience that frame—how much presence, resolution, and time we can enter within it.

We discovered the following:

- **Brain waves are not just signals—they are selectors.**
  Your dominant frequency determines how fluidly you move through time, how richly you experience each moment, and how coherently your awareness functions.
- **Gamma is our intended state.**
  Gamma lets you *enter* frames more fully. In gamma each frame becomes a world—saturated, meaningful, and multidimensional.

- **Clarity is the new intelligence.**
  Not how fast you think but how harmoniously your awareness integrates emotion, memory, perception, and intention.
- **You are not stuck in time—you are tuning it.**
  Just like a radio dial selects a frequency, your consciousness selects a timeline. And in gamma, it doesn't just choose–it *conducts.*
- **Neurochemistry is the tuner.**
  Whether it's serotonin's calm, dopamine's drive, or ayahuasca's purge, your chemistry acts like the filter that determines which brain wave states you can access and which experiences you're ready to perceive.
- **Awareness is a feedback loop.**
  Your vibration shapes the field. The field reshapes you. Like cymatics, the moment responds to your internal tone, and the echo becomes your next frame.

And most importantly, **your brain was built for gamma coherence**. The CORE state isn't a peak you reach. It's a frequency you *remember.*

Now that we've seen how awareness selects, sculpts, and resolves each moment, a deeper question arises: **What happens after the frame collapses?**

What happens to the tone you emit, the vibration you leave behind? Does it simply fade? Or does it echo?

Chapter 5 explores this next layer of the CR model.
Where frequency becomes feedback.
Where every collapsed moment leaves a signature.
And where those signatures begin to shape what comes next.

This is not the old idea of karma as judgment.

This is karma as **vibrational momentum**—the resonant wake of your consciousness, returning not to punish but to harmonize.

What you send out is what you navigate back into. Each thought, word, and act becomes a tone in the field. And in an entangled, recursive universe, those tones return, not because the universe keeps score but because **you are still vibrating**.

In this view karma is not cosmic bookkeeping. It's your own field, played back.

So in chapter 5 we'll see how trauma loops, relationship patterns, and déjà vu may all stem from recursive, nested echoes; you inherit momentum—from your ancestors, your choices, and even your unconscious tone; and most importantly you are not trapped by your past signal.

You can't outrun karma.

But you can **retune it**.

Let's step deeper into this field of echoes, where consciousness doesn't just shape the now.

It calls forth the next.

5

THE ECHO OF
YOUR TONE

*A man is the whole encyclopedia of facts. The creation of a
thousand forests is in one acorn, and Egypt, Greece, Rome, Gaul,
Britain, America, lie folded already in the first man. Epoch after
epoch, camp, kingdom, empire, republic, democracy, are merely
the application of his manifold spirit to the manifold world.*
—RALPH WALDO EMERSON

KARMA AS THE VIBRATIONAL ECHO OF ACTION

The ship was steady now. It hovered in low Earth orbit, suspended above the swirl of continents and clouds. But something had changed in the crew, not outside but inside. Their minds were no longer fragmented across timelines, distracted by static or reruns of thought. Each had learned to tune awareness with precision. They could now feel the field.

And with that sensitivity came something unexpected.

Not just clarity.
But continuity.

They began to notice echoes. Moments they had once dismissed as coincidence revealed deeper symmetry. A passing thought returned in a stranger's voice. A memory looped back through the present as déjà vu. An unresolved conflict took form in a new encounter—different face, same tone.

The ship had never truly *pushed* forward.

It had been pulled—drawn by the gravity of their own unresolved vibrations. Every choice, every intention, every frequency they'd once emitted had left a trail. And now those echoes were the coordinates.

Karma wasn't a judge—it was a map.

A propulsion system powered not by thrust but by resonance. Their journey had not just been through space. It had been through their own vibrational field—looping through patterns left unfinished, retracing harmonics in need of retuning, closing loops opened by ancestors and lifetimes long past.

They hadn't just mastered navigation through time.
They had entered a new layer:
Return.

In most spiritual traditions, karma is understood as a kind of cosmic justice system—an invisible balance sheet of deeds stretched across lifetimes. Good actions are believed to bring rewards, while harmful ones are said to bring suffering. But in CR, karma is not a system of moral accounting. It is a phenomenon of resonance.

Every action you take, every word you speak, and every thought you generate carries a vibrational tone. These tones ripple into the CORE field of reality like waves in a pool. And because the universe itself is built from fields and feedback loops, those waves return, not as punishment or reward but as harmonic response. A reverberation.

Reality in the CR view is not fixed and separate from you; it is a responsive medium, something malleable and shaped. When you emit a frequency, the universe responds in kind. You collapse a moment through your tone of awareness, and that moment, in turn, shapes the next frame of your reality. This is how karma operates, not as retribution but as vibrational echo.

The past, in this view, is not something you leave behind. It is more accurate to say you are riding the momentum of past frequencies. Just like the Saturn crew who didn't move forward through space but were pulled by collapsed probabilities, you are not being pushed linearly through time. You are being drawn forward by the resonance of prior frames. Your reality is sculpted not only by what you do but also by the tone you carry into each moment. In this way karma becomes a pattern—a vibrational momentum that gathers force over time. And like all patterns, it can be shifted—but only by changing the tone.

ENTANGLED MOMENTUM

In a quantum field where everything is connected, your tone never exists in isolation. You are not just echoing your own actions. You are also entangled with the frequencies of others—your parents, your ancestors, your culture, and the larger collective field. These influences are vibrationally present in your field.

Much of what you experience in life may not originate from your own personal choices, but it still moves through you. You inherit not just physical traits or beliefs but also energetic momentum—vibrational tendencies shaped by your lineage and environment.

This doesn't mean you are powerless. On the contrary it means you are profoundly responsible. The experiences you encounter are not random. They are harmonic. They align with the frequencies you emit and the inherited patterns you have yet to retune.

In this view you are the living intersection of countless vibrations—some ancient, some new. But you are not just a passive receiver. You are a conscious participant. You are the tuning fork.

Like the acorn Emerson wrote about, within you lives the potential of forests not yet formed. But those forests are not guaranteed. They emerge based on how you cultivate and direct the tone of your consciousness. You carry the echoes of those who came before, but you also hold the power to alter the frequency moving forward.

This is the deeper meaning of karmic responsibility, not as moral debt but as vibrational authorship. You cannot always control what you inherit, but you can decide how to respond, how to tune your field, and how to change the pattern for those who come next.

LOOPS AND RECURSIONS

If karma is vibrational momentum, then loops are the shapes that momentum tends to follow. They are the patterns that repeat, not because the universe is punishing you but because your field has not yet shifted. These loops are seen as vibrational echoes—reverberations of frequency that have not yet been harmonized.

This is why you may find yourself in the same kind of relationship again and again, even if the people change. Its why old traumas seem to resurface in new forms, why similar challenges arise at different points in your life, and why déjà vu feels like a glitch in the filmstrip of reality. These are not accidents. They are recurring experiences that emerge from disharmonized tone. Patterns repeat across time but not in a straight line—in nested, mirrored ways. A conversation can mirror a childhood wound. A decision made today can echo across generations. Each moment is a microcosm of the whole—a chance to glimpse the deeper pattern and shift it.

At the heart of these loops is a principle called **fractal recurrence**. In chapter 3 we explored how nature is built on fractals—geometric patterns that repeat at every level of scale. The branching of neurons mirrors the structure of galaxies. Blood vessels echo the veins of leaves. Even Romanesco broccoli spirals in perfect self-similar curves. These aren't just visual curiosities—they're structural signatures of resonance. What repeats in form also repeats in frequency. In the same way that patterns in nature repeat at different scales—from galaxies to seashells—so, too, do life's emotional and spiritual patterns. A wound in childhood might reappear in your career, your friendships, or your parenting. The form may change, but the frequency remains the same until it is retuned.

This repetition is not a flaw in the system. It *is* the system. Reality is structured like a fractal—self-similar across scales. Your individual patterns are nested within generational patterns, which are nested within cultural patterns, which are nested within the collective human field. Loops exist because fields seek coherence. A discordant frequency will keep surfacing in new forms until it is brought into harmony.

This relates to the principle of **entrainment**, where vibrating systems naturally synchronize when they share proximity. But **fractal recurrence** adds a deeper layer: These patterns don't just synchronize— they *reappear*, echoing across time and scale. An unresolved emotional tone might entrain with your partner in the present, but it can also replay within your family's generational drama, your culture's inherited myths, or even the collective trauma of humanity.

Entrainment explains how frequencies align. **Fractal recurrence** explains why they keep returning—until coherence is achieved.

Generational cycles are a powerful example of this. Often, we unconsciously inherit the unresolved echoes of our ancestors—traumas that were never processed, patterns that were never completed. These can show up as fears we can't explain, habits we struggle to break, or emotional themes that haunt our lineage. Entire generations may be stuck in disharmony from the CORE field, like a warped record on repeat.

But just as you can inherit a loop, you can also resolve it. And when you do, you don't just heal yourself—**you shift the resonance of your entire lineage**. Perhaps your ancestors are looking to you now to lift them up.

In the CR view, life is not linear. It is recursive. Each moment is both a repetition and an invitation—a chance to notice the loop and choose a new tone. The universe will keep echoing the same frame until you collapse it differently.

This is not fate. It's feedback. And it points to one of CR's most empowering insights:

When you change the frequency of your awareness, you change the trajectory not only of your life but of your ancestors as well.

SELF-RELIANCE AND VIBRATIONAL RESPONSIBILITY

Karma is not something you can outrun, escape, or bypass. It is the tone of your field, and wherever you go, that field goes with you.

You might change your job, your relationship, or your location, but if the frequency remains unchanged, the pattern will reappear in a new form. This is why healing doesn't come from external shifts alone. It comes from internal retuning.

Self-reliance, then, is not just about independence. It's about energetic accountability. You are responsible for the tone you carry—and therefore for the reality that tone attracts and sustains. This doesn't mean you are to blame for every hardship. But it does mean you are a participant in the field that shapes your life.

As Emerson once wrote, "Do not go where the path may lead, go instead where there is no path and leave a trail."

True self-reliance means not just following inherited frequencies but consciously shaping new ones. It is the courage to collapse old loops and emit a new signal—one that reshapes the path not only ahead but behind you as well.

Hardships or obstacles, in this view, are not enemies. They are invitations. As Machiavelli wrote, "Without doubt, princes become great when they overcome difficulties and hurdles put in their path. When fortune wants to advance a new prince... She creates enemies for him, making them launch campaigns against him so that he is compelled to overcome them and climb higher on the ladder that they have brought him." In other words hardships are not a deviation from your path—it is the path.

Difficulties arise in our lives because they are harmonically related to the tones in your field. They are not there to defeat you. They are there to give you a chance to elevate and retune. **Each obstacle is a vibrational test: Can you meet it with a higher frequency than the one that summoned it?**
This is why we face repeated hardships; we will continue to experience them by design until we retune.

This is the essence of vibrational responsibility. It means no longer helplessly waiting for life to change. It means taking action and responsibility. It means breaking cycles. And it means recognizing that every experience, especially the painful ones, is feedback from a universe that loves you and wants you to harmonize.

Personal growth is not about transcending difficulty. It is about transmuting it. When you meet hardship with clarity, presence, and elevated tone, the loop ends. The pattern changes. The field evolves.
And with it, so do you.

HOLOGRAPHIC KARMA

In many traditions there is a recognition that divine truth is woven into every part of creation. The whole can be seen in the part. The eternal can be known in the present. "The kingdom of God is within you" (Luke 17:21, New King James Version). This is the basis of what CR calls **holographic karma**: the idea that each moment contains the whole pattern of your life, just as a drop of water contains the memory of the ocean.

You might notice it in something as simple as an argument with a loved one, where a single moment of frustration carries the emotional tone of years, even generations. In that flash of reaction, your childhood patterns, your parents' wounds, and even ancestral echoes are all present. The entire karmic thread is folded into that moment, inviting awareness, healing, and retuning. A chance to meet the loop with awareness and to retune. Fractal recurrence.

For if God created a universe of order and meaning, then even the smallest experience carries divine intelligence. Nothing is random. Everything is meaningful. As the Bible says, "Even the very hairs of your head are all numbered" (Luke 12:7, King James Version).

Your field is the place where God's truth meets your free will. You are given the freedom to choose, but you are not left without feedback. That feedback is karma, not as punishment but as a reverberated response. It is how the universe teaches. It is how God calls us back into harmony.

To understand holographic karma is to realize that healing doesn't have to take years or lifetimes. It can happen in an instant—because every moment holds the pattern, and every pattern can be retuned. With enough awareness, forgiveness, and surrender, even the heaviest karmic echo can dissolve in the presence of divine grace. We all have a chance. Always.

This is not just personal. It is redemptive. When you change the pattern in yourself, you free others entangled in it—past, present, and future. You become a vessel of restoration. You collapse not just your own suffering but the suffering that once moved through your lineage.

In this way karma is not a burden to carry—it is a chance to free yourself and find harmony.

THE RETURN PATH

Karma is not fate.
It is not judgment.
It is resonance.

You do not live in a universe of blind cause and effect but in one of intelligent response. A relational universe, where the tone of your being draws forth the shape of your reality.

This means nothing is random. Every experience is either a reflection of your current frequency or an opportunity to elevate it. The field is always responding to you, not to what you say you want but to what you vibrate.

This is the invitation to stop waiting for the world to change and instead become the kind of field that changes the world. To take responsibility not as burden but as creative power. To recognize that within you is the ability to shift entire patterns—personal, generational, and even collective.

And this is where grace meets frequency.

You are not evolving alone. You are being guided back into coherence—again and again—until your tone becomes a match for the harmony that made you.

Karma, then, is not the weight of your past.

It is the echo of your becoming.

6

VIBRATIONAL CLEANSING

The first and greatest victory is to conquer yourself.
—PLATO

COHERENCE AS CREATIVE AUTHORITY

The Saturn crew floated in low Earth orbit, gazing down at the blue swirl of continents and clouds.

As the days passed, each member began noticing how their experience of reality shifted in response to their inner tone. When they felt anxious, the ship's systems responded sluggishly. When their thoughts scattered, time fragmented. But when they centered themselves—when breath, emotion, and awareness moved in harmony—the environment began to open. Guidance became clear. Decisions arrived without strain. And time, once rigid, began to stretch.

They were discovering a truth known to sages long before astronauts: *Coherence is power.*

Coherence is the foundation of creative authority. When your body, mind, and emotions are aligned, your field becomes stable. And a stable field doesn't just receive reality—it shapes it. You no longer collapse frames reactively. You collapse them deliberately, with clarity.

This is not achieved by force. *You cannot bully the universe into harmony.* Instead, the field responds to resonance. Your signal must match the structure you hope to create. This is why Plato's words still hold: The greatest victory is self-mastery. When you align your inner world, the outer one follows.

The power to shape reality is not found in effort or force. It is found in frequency and, specifically, in coherence. When your internal systems are out of sync, your field becomes fragmented. And fragmented fields cannot shape reality with precision. You may take action, but it won't collapse clean frames. You may speak your desires, but the tone behind your words will be scattered. Reality doesn't respond to your goals—it responds to your signal. And your signal only becomes powerful when it is coherent.

Coherence is the alignment of your inner systems—mental, emotional, physical, and spiritual—into a single, resonant tone. When coherence is present, your field becomes a tuning fork. You don't push reality. You resonate with it. The moment begins to respond not to your effort but to your presence.

Incoherence, by contrast, is noise. You might want healing but harbor resentment. You might speak of love but carry shame. These crosscurrents cancel each other out like waves crashing against themselves. This is why many people feel stuck, not because they lack desire but because their field is divided. Their force is scattered.

The ancient world had words for coherence, even if they didn't use the term. In religious texts we find phrases such as "singleness of heart" or "renewal of the mind." These are not just moral teachings.

They are vibrational instructions. When the heart is single and the mind is renewed, the signal is clean. The field is strong.

A coherent electromagnetic field—like the one generated by a heart in alignment—can entrain surrounding systems. Studies in neuro-cardiology have shown that when a person enters a state of grati-tude, love, or compassion, the heart rhythm becomes smooth and harmonic.[1] The brain begins to synchronize.[2] Stress patterns dis-solve. And more than that, the external environment begins to shift. People nearby begin to match the signal.[3] Reality reorganizes around the coherent tone.

Therefore, coherence is not just a state of well-being—it is creative authority. It is the vibrational condition necessary to collapse harmo-nious frames. Belief and emotion are not passive—they are architec-tural tones. They sculpt what form will emerge.

As discussed in chapter 4, **gamma** is the highest state of coherence. It is when the brain enters full-spectrum synchronization—across hemispheres, across lobes—operating not as fragmented modules but as a unified field. In gamma consciousness resonates with the CORE field itself. This state is not just mentally alert—it is vibra-tionally aligned. Mystics, healers, and visionaries often report gamma as the frequency of insight, unity, and transcendence.

This is why belief matters, not in the shallow sense of positive thinking but as a frequency generator. Belief is the inner waveform that deter-mines which possibilities stabilize into form. If you believe the world is unsafe, your field filters for threat. If you believe you are unworthy, your tone collapses frames that mirror rejection.

Your outer world echoes the tone of your inner world, and **karma** com-pounds these tones over time. As explored in chapter 5, karma is not punishment or reward—it is vibrational **momentum**. Each thought, action, or belief emits a tone. And that tone either reinforces coherence or prolongs dissonance. Over time these vibrational patterns solidify into experience. You live inside the echo of your own field.

Emotion deepens this process. Emotion is energy in motion, and it carries the weight of your field. It adds charge to your beliefs and accelerates the collapse of frames. Love, awe, forgiveness, and joy elevate the field. They stretch time, open perception, and attract coherent outcomes. Fear, shame, and rage fragment the field. They are low states of awareness. They compress time, narrow vision, and collapse jagged, unstable realities.

This is why emotional mastery is important—it's about command. Not denying emotion but learning to stabilize your field so emotion flows *through* you, not *over* you. To feel fully, without becoming fragmented. When you transmute anger or grief, it's not suppression—it's evolution. You reassert sovereignty over your signal. You clear distortion. And in doing so, you unlock access to higher frames of awareness, where creation flows cleanly again.

Marcus Aurelius, the Stoic philosopher and Roman emperor, understood this. He wrote, "The soul becomes dyed with the color of its thoughts." His words are not just moral instruction—they are vibrational truth. Directing the mind is not about denial. It is about resonance. When you direct your inner tone with clarity and awareness, you reshape what becomes possible around you.

The Stoics, like the mystics, practiced coherence long before we had the vocabulary of frequency. To "make yourself simpler and better," as Marcus wrote, is to clear the noise so that the signal of the soul can emerge cleanly through the field.

In the CR view, creative authority is the natural result of vibrational integrity. You do not need to dominate the world to shape it. You only need to become the kind of field that harmonizes with what you desire. When your intention, emotion, and belief align into one coherent signal, the universe does not resist you—it responds to you.

Let's reorient ourselves using the steps from prior chapters.

- **Step 1:** You Choose the Frame (Chapter 2)—Just like a film director selects a shot, your awareness chooses a moment from the infinite stream of possibility.
  - When you're anxious or distracted, you collapse frames, reactively flipping through reality like someone channel surfing without paying attention.
  - When you're focused and present, you select frames with intention—like a photographer waiting for perfect light, choosing not just what's next but what matters.
  - *You are the one collapsing the moment into being.*

- **Step 2:** You Shape the Frame with Vibration (Chapter 3)— Once you've selected the moment, your inner frequency gives it texture and tone—just like a cymatic vibration shapes a pattern in sand or water.
  - If your internal state is chaotic or fearful, the frame becomes jagged, incoherent.
  - If your state is loving, calm, or grateful, that same moment crystallizes into beauty, symmetry, and depth.
  - *Your vibration determines what the frame becomes.*

- **Step 3:** You Control the Resolution of the Frame (Chapter 4)—Your brain wave sets the "frame rate" of your consciousness—like adjusting how many stills your camera captures per second. The faster the brain wave, the more frames you stitch into each moment—and the deeper your experience becomes. Your brain's frequency sets the clarity and richness of what you experience.

- Low frequencies (theta and delta) are like blurry photos. They're important for dreaming and restoration, but not great for clear perception.
- High frequencies (especially gamma) are like shooting in 4k, ultra-HD. You see into each frame with greater detail.
- *Gamma awareness is like stepping into a slow-motion, high-definition version of reality—where everything becomes luminous, layered, and alive.*

And in this response, time bends. Space reorganizes. New outcomes appear, not by luck but by universal law.

DAILY PRACTICES FOR RAISING FREQUENCY

Understanding frequency is only the beginning.
Living it is the work.
Coherence is the path. Gamma is the result.

Here's how we get there:

You can study vibration, coherence, and the laws of consciousness for a lifetime. But without practice—without integration—it remains conceptual. Raising your frequency is not an idea you hold in your mind. It is a lifestyle. A discipline. A daily recalibration of your inner tone.

This chapter is the pivot point from understanding to action.

Everything that follows depends on it. Because the truth is, **you cannot collapse new frames with an old frequency.**

The daily practices below are not rituals to perform out of obligation. They are **vibrational technologies**—tools to stabilize your field, elevate your awareness, and access the deeper structure of time itself.

144

Over time these practices help entrain the system toward gamma—a state of brain wave coherence associated with peak awareness, compassion, and insight.

Each is simple in form but profound in effect. Use them not as tasks but as invitations. And remember, **mastery is not about never falling out of coherence. It's about how quickly you return to it.**

BREATH–RHYTHM IS REALITY

Your breath is the most accessible and immediate tool for altering your frequency. It is the bridge between the conscious and unconscious, the voluntary and the involuntary. And because of this, it is also the bridge between your awareness and your field.

Most people breathe unconsciously—shallow, rapid, and erratic. We never truly exhale all the air in our lungs, and the old air stays trapped, stagnant.

These patterns often reflect and reinforce a state of incoherence. The breath becomes jagged when the mind is anxious, tight when the body is tense, and suppressed when emotions are locked away.

But when you take conscious control of your breath—when you slow it, smooth it, and make it rhythmic—you send a powerful signal to your entire system: **We are safe. We are present. We are coherent.**

Scientific studies have confirmed this. Rhythmic breathing activates the **parasympathetic nervous system**, reduces cortisol, and synchronizes the brain and heart.[4] Research from institutions such as **Stanford**, **Harvard**, and the **HeartMath Institute** shows that even five minutes of coherent breathing can lead to

- increased heart rate variability,[5]
- reduced amygdala activity (fear response),[6]

- greater prefrontal cortex activation (conscious regulation),[7] and in some cases,
- elevated **gamma wave activity**, especially when paired with gratitude or meditation.[8]

Rhythmic breathing creates rhythmic brain waves. It entrains the heart to the breath and the nervous system to the heart. Over time this internal harmony becomes your new baseline. You begin to default to calm awareness. You begin to respond to life rather than react to it.

A foundational CR breathing practice is this:

- Inhale for a count of five. Inhale positivity and possibility.
- Exhale for a count of five. Exhale negativity and your intention.
- Continue for five minutes.
- Focus your awareness on the heart as you breathe.
- Feel gratitude—or simply feel.
- Inhale completely to fill your lungs.
- Exhale completely to expel stagnant air.

This practice isn't just about calming down.

It's about tuning up.

The breath is not just a tool for relaxation—it is a metronome for your field.

And when your breath becomes coherent, your reality follows.

SOUND—SHAPING THE FIELD THROUGH VIBRATION

Sound is not simply entertainment. It is structure. Every sound you allow into your environment, and every tone you emit through your voice, is a sculptor of your field. In CR sound is understood as one of the most direct ways to modify your vibrational architecture.

As we explored in chapter 3, **sound doesn't just influence matter—it organizes it**. Cymatic experiments show how different frequencies create specific geometric patterns in physical media. The more harmonic the frequency, the more coherent the structure.

One frequency stands out across traditions and modern research: **432 Hz**. Often called the *natural tuning*, 432 Hz resonates with the geometry of the universe, the vibration of Earth (Schumann resonance), and even the patterns in sacred architecture.

Music tuned to 432 Hz has been shown to reduce anxiety, slow the heart rate, and promote synchronization between brain hemispheres. In CR this tuning is understood not as superstition but as **resonant alignment**—sound that supports the integrity of your field.

The reason for this is simple: Sound is frequency made audible. And frequency is what collapses frames. Therefore, sound can either disrupt or reinforce the integrity of your reality.

When you listen to chaotic, dissonant, or aggressive music, your nervous system tightens. Your brain waves fragment. Your field destabilizes. When you expose yourself to sacred sounds—tones, mantras, singing bowls, or deeply harmonic music—you bring the field back into resonance.

But beyond listening, your own voice is the most powerful instrument. Humming, chanting, singing, and toning are ancient tools because they work. They resonate through the bones of the body, activate the vagus nerve, and send harmonic feedback through the energetic field.

Mantras and prayers are not magic because of their language. They are magic because of their vibration. Repetition is not mindless—it is rhythmic alignment. When you repeat a sacred phrase or vowel sound, you are not just saying words. You are shaping structure.

Studies show that chanting and harmonic vocalization can increase **gamma wave activity**, particularly when practiced with intention and heart-centered emotion.[9] In this state the brain enters a unified rhythm—across hemispheres, across systems[10]—where perception sharpens, intuition deepens, and the field becomes coherent.

This is not just mental clarity—it is vibrational elevation. **Sound can lift you into gamma.**

Here's a daily practice:

- Begin or end your day with five minutes of vocal toning.
- Hum a single note that feels natural. Let it rise and fall organically.
- Or repeat a sacred syllable such as "Om," "Amen," or even a word of your own personal significance—slowly, with full attention.
- Observe how the body responds. Notice where tension dissolves. Feel your tone settle.

Through this you begin to realize your voice is not for information. It is for creation.

SILENCE—THE PRESENCE BENEATH THE NOISE

Silence is often misunderstood. In a world saturated with stimulation, silence is seen as a void—something to fill. But in CR silence is sacred. It is not the absence of sound. It is the presence of source.

Silence is the vibrational baseline. It is the stillness that precedes every waveform. Just as every sound emerges from silence, every moment emerges from still awareness. To spend time in silence is to return to the origin point. It is to steep your consciousness in unshaped potential.

This is not merely about "quiet time." It is about entering the space beneath mental chatter. In silence your attention detaches from thought-forms. Your awareness returns to being itself.

And from that place, your frequency recalibrates.

Silence is where gamma begins.

When the external noise falls away, the brain's systems can synchronize. Studies have shown that deep states of silent presence—particularly in meditation or mindful stillness—are associated with the emergence of **gamma brain waves**, the frequency of integration, coherence, and elevated consciousness. In silence the mind stops reacting and begins resonating.

STILLNESS TECHNOLOGIES—MEDITATION, FLOATING, AND THE DEEP RESET

In a world of constant input, stillness is not accidental—it must be cultivated. And two of the most powerful tools for accessing vibrational stillness are meditation and sensory deprivation.

Meditation is not just mental discipline. It is vibrational tuning. When practiced regularly, it entrains the brain into coherent frequencies—lowering beta, calming the nervous system, and opening the doorway to alpha, theta, and eventually gamma states. Each breath becomes a reset. Each moment of nondoing becomes a return to the uncollapsed field.

Meditation is not about silencing the mind—it is about learning to rest *beneath* it.

But even deeper silence can be accessed when all sensory input is reduced. This is the gift of **floating**—or sensory deprivation. In a float tank, all external light, sound, and even gravity-based sensation are removed. The body disappears. The external world vanishes. And what's left is pure internal resonance.

In these environments the mind is invited into profound introspection and neural synchronization. Studies have shown that floating enhances theta and gamma activity; lowers cortisol, depression, and anxiety; and can unlock altered states of unity, clarity, and timelessness.[11, 12, 13]

Whether through meditation or floating, the aim is the same: *to return to the baseline frequency of presence. To release distortion. To recalibrate the field.*

These practices are not escapes from reality—they are retuning of the self *so you can reenter reality with coherence.*

Make them part of your vibrational hygiene.

- Daily meditation, even for five minutes
- Occasional float sessions to reset deeper layers of the nervous system
- Silence not just as an absence but as a **vibrational chamber of renewal**

This is also the space of reflection. Without distraction you begin to observe the terrain of your own mind.

Explore it.

Notice your thoughts, your emotions, your habits.
Not to judge them but to meet them with awareness.
Self-reflection is not indulgent—it is vibrational hygiene.

Learning to be comfortable in your own presence and silence can be difficult, especially in a world of endless stimulus. But the truth is, **you cannot truly love yourself if you cannot sit with yourself.**

In silence the noise dissolves. The interference disappears.
And what remains is the **clean signal of your soul.**

Make space for silence every day, not just once but in small rituals.

- One minute of silence before meals
- A few breaths of silence before responding in conversation
- Five minutes of silent stillness in the morning, before looking at a screen
- A walk without music, podcast, or phone, just presence

Silence is not passive. It is presence.

And presence is where coherence—and gamma—are born.

INTENTION–DIRECTING THE FIELD BEFORE ACTION

Every frame of reality begins with a tone. And every tone begins with intention.

Intention is not just a mental wish. It is a vibrational command. Before you act, speak, or move, your field has already broadcast your tone. That tone becomes the filter through which your moment unfolds.

This is why CR views intention as essential. You don't get what you want. You get what you broadcast. And what you broadcast is often unspoken, hidden in your subconscious beliefs, your emotional state, and the quality of your attention.

And what you broadcast isn't just what you think in the moment—it's the echo of your subconscious field.

The **subconscious** is not a passive storage unit. It is a frequency amplifier. It doesn't filter or question—it simply absorbs and radiates what the conscious mind consumes. If you watch violence, the subconscious thinks you want to see more violence. This is why patterns persist even when you "know better." Beliefs held subconsciously are more powerful than those stated consciously—because they are vibrationally consistent.

Clearing is not suppression. It's transmutation.

When you notice fear, resentment, or shame in your field, don't deny it. **Acknowledge it. Feel it fully. Then move it.** Breath, sound, tears, movement, and even conscious visualization—these are tools not just for emotion but for **energy hygiene**.

Imagine your body as an instrument. You can't play a pure tone through strings choked with tension.

Release allows resonance.

Even a brief practice can change your entire broadcast.

- Name the emotion.
- Breathe into where you feel it in your body.
- Exhale through the mouth, as if blowing it out.
- Use intention: *I release this tone. I retune to clarity.*

When you clear your field, you don't just shift your experience—you lighten the collective. Your tone affects others, just as theirs affects you. **We are entangled fields**, constantly exchanging frequency. Clearing your energy is not selfish. It's service.

To work with intention is to take responsibility for your **internal broadcast system**. That means actively noticing what unspoken signals are operating beneath your words and, when needed, clearing them.

Setting intention is the art of aligning the signal before the frame collapses. It is not control. It is calibration.

Here's a daily practice:

Before beginning any meaningful task—writing, working, meeting, or even eating—pause for five seconds.

Breathe once.

Ask, "What tone am I carrying into this task?"

If the tone is fear, resentment, or distraction, don't force it away. Breathe again. Set a clear intention: I choose to enter with clarity. I choose to speak with integrity. I choose to hold love.

Then move forward.

You don't have to be perfect. But you must be deliberate. Intention gives the moment a shape before it forms.

HEART FOCUS—ACCESSING THE PORTAL OF COHERENCE

The heart is not only the emotional center of the body—it is also its energetic conductor. It generates the strongest electromagnetic field of any organ and sends more information to the brain than the brain sends to the heart.

In CR the heart is the portal to coherence.

When the heart is in a smooth, sine wave rhythm—such as during moments of gratitude or compassion—the entire system enters alignment.[14] Brain waves synchronize. Breathing slows. Immune function improves. But more than this, reality becomes clearer.[15] You gain access to higher frames. And at the peak of that coherence lies **gamma**—the brain wave state of unity, insight, and heightened perception.[16] When intention is heart-centered, and the field is clear, the brain begins to operate in full-spectrum synchrony.

Gamma is not achieved through effort but through alignment. It is the vibrational signature of an integrated system—mind, body, heart, and field all resonating as one.

Over time this calibration leads to coherence. And from coherence gamma becomes possible.

This is how deliberate living reshapes your neural architecture, not just emotionally or spiritually but biologically.

Studies on long-term meditators and heart-focused practices show that repeated coherence cultivates **neuroplasticity**—the brain's ability to rewire its structure and function in response to experience.[17]

When you live with deliberate intention, you're not just changing your day—you're training your nervous system to stabilize a new frequency.

PRESENT COHERENCE—THE CR RULE FOR TIME

"Learn from the past, but do not let it torment you.
Wonder about the future, but do not let it paralyze you."

This is the CR approach to time.

Most people live scattered across timelines—pushed by memory, pulled by anticipation. But true coherence can only occur in the now because only the present holds the power to collapse frames.

The past is real but only as momentum. If you dwell in it, you revive frequencies that no longer belong. The future is real but only as potential. If you obsess over it, you fracture the moment and destabilize the field.

Presence is the one place where intention, emotion, and awareness can meet.

Here's a daily practice:

Choose a reminder—a bracelet, a phone background, a phrase—to call you back to the present.

When you feel anxious, say aloud, "I return to now. I collapse this frame with peace and love in my heart."

Let the moment become your frame, not just your backdrop.

Presence is where power lives. And coherence is what keeps you there.

In states of deep coherence, especially **gamma**, time begins to stretch. You experience more reality in less clock-time. This is not imagination; it's perceptual dilation. Higher-frequency awareness collapses more frames per second, creating the sensation of spaciousness, clarity, and flow.

In these states **karmic momentum** can also be reshaped. When you act from gamma, you're not operating from old loops—you're broadcasting a purified tone, free from reactive patterns. This breaks resonance with old timelines. It allows new outcomes to emerge, not by force but by frequency.

The present isn't just a place of peace. It's the **portal of transformation**.

From here, you can alter karmic patterns, accelerate growth, and expand time itself.

Each breath you take with awareness, each sound you make with care, each moment of silence you honor—each one is a path to a higher timeline. A step into a more resonant version of you.

Presence is not stillness. It is power.

And in gamma, presence becomes momentum—the kind that bends karma and stretches time.

DETOX AND PURIFICATION

The body is not separate from your consciousness.

It is not a shell that carries your awareness—it is awareness, crystallized. It is your field made dense.

Every cell, every organ, every breath you take is not just biological—it is vibrational. You are a frequency being in a physical form. And that form—this body—is not just along for the ride. It is your interface. It is how you transmit and receive energy. It is how you collapse frames.

Detox is meant to honor the body as a sacred instrument—to clear the static that blocks your signal. Because your ability to access higher frequencies is directly tied to the clarity of your vessel.

When the body is cluttered—with toxins, processed chemicals, heavy metals, stimulants, and inflammation—the field becomes murky. The signal gets garbled. Awareness feels dull. Intuition fades. The timelines you collapse feel limited, chaotic, or distorted, not because you aren't spiritual but because your instrument is out of tune.

This happens because your **body is not separate from your awareness—it is the interface** through which awareness collapses frames.

Think of your body as both antenna and amplifier. The cleaner the antenna, the clearer the signal it can receive and transmit.

When the body is burdened by toxins, processed foods, chemical stimulants, or chronic inflammation, several things occur simultaneously.

- **Electrical conductivity decreases:** Cellular communication becomes slower or fragmented, which disrupts coherence between the nervous system, heart, and brain.
- **Brain wave patterns destabilize:** High inflammation and poor gut health directly affect the production of neurotransmitters and coherence of brain rhythms, making it harder to reach higher states such as **gamma**.
- **Intuition becomes muffled:** The energetic field becomes chaotic and dissonant, clouding the clarity needed to receive subtle information.
- **The collapse of frames becomes reactive, not intentional:** Instead of consciously selecting timelines with awareness, your field reverts to looping old frequencies driven by physical discomfort, fatigue, or stress.

In CR the body is not an obstacle to consciousness—it is the vessel of it. When the body is in tune, awareness sharpens, the signal strengthens, and the **timelines you collapse become more aligned, coherent, and expansive**.

This is why detox and purification are not side quests. They are central to the path.

THE PINEAL GLAND: PORTAL OF PERCEPTION

At the center of the brain lies a small, pine-cone-shaped gland—the pineal. For centuries mystics such as René Descartes have called it the *seat of the soul.* The third-eye chakra.

EXHIBIT 6A

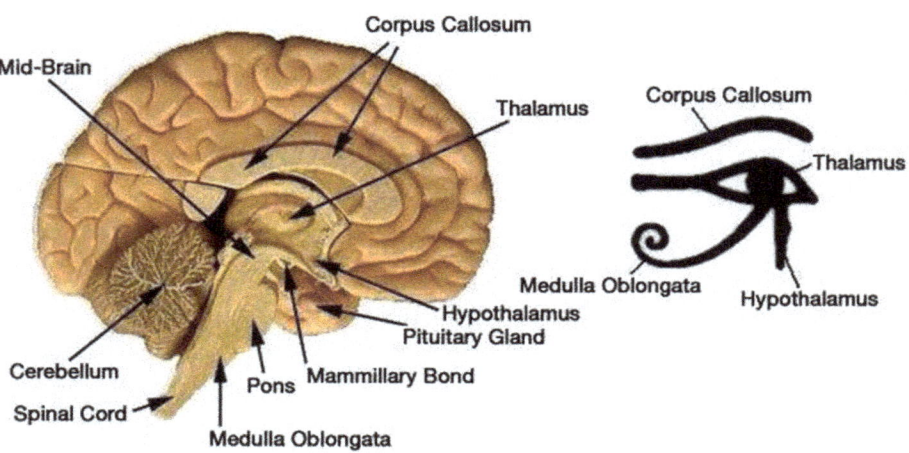

Above: *A cross section of the human brain reveals a remarkable resemblance between the pineal region—including the thalamus, corpus callosum, and hypothalamus—and the ancient Egyptian Eye of Horus. In Egyptian cosmology the Eye represented protection, perception, and divine insight. In modern neuroscience the pineal gland is associated with circadian rhythm and—some argue—inner vision. Whether coincidence or deep symbolic intuition, this alignment suggests that ancient cultures may have encoded spiritual and anatomical knowledge into their sacred symbology.*

There are compelling visual comparisons between the ancient Egyptian Eye of Horus symbol and the anatomical structure of the human brain, particularly the region encompassing the pineal gland. These parallels suggest that ancient cultures may have recognized more than symbolic truth—they may have understood the pineal as a literal **center of perception**. The alignment between the Eye of Horus and midline brain anatomy (the thalamus, hypothalamus, corpus callosum, and pineal) hints at an ancient awareness of the gland's metaphysical purpose.

The pineal is photoreceptive, electromagnetic, and piezoelectric. It is designed to receive light and transduce subtle energy into perception. But when it is calcified—by fluoride, processed food, heavy metals, and chronic stress—its function begins to fade.

What makes the pineal gland so extraordinary is not just its function but its *location*.

It's buried deep within the brain's core, surrounded by cerebrospinal fluid, structurally isolated in darkness, and yet it responds to light. It has **no direct connection to the outside world**.

And yet it *responds to light*.

This is bizarre. A light-sensitive gland, locked in total darkness. No other part of the body functions this way.

How does it know when the Sun rises? How does it register changes in the light spectrum throughout the day?

The answer lies in a delicate and highly coordinated chain: The eyes absorb light, transmit signals through the **retinohypothalamic tract**, and relay that data to the **suprachiasmatic nucleus**, which governs circadian rhythm. That information is then passed to the pineal.

In other words light travels through your body to reach an organ that was once an eye.

Yes, the pineal gland is *literally a vestigial third eye.*

It has photoreceptive cells similar to those in the retina.

It is electromagnetic, responding to geomagnetic fields.

And it is piezoelectric, meaning it converts mechanical pressure (like vibrational energy) into electrical signals.

This makes it a unique transducer—capable of converting **light, frequency, and subtle energy into conscious experience**.

But when the pineal is calcified—through fluoride exposure, processed foods, heavy metals, electromagnetic field (EMF) pollution, and chronic stress—it becomes less sensitive, less active, less coherent.

Intuition dulls. Vivid dreaming fades. Inner sight closes.

It's not that your spirit is gone. It's that the *receiver* is out of tune.

And the pineal gland is a **structural antenna for divine signal**.

It is not symbolic—it is literal. A crystalline, piezoelectric transducer designed to receive subtle energetic information and convert it into perception, intuition, and coherence.

As discussed in chapter 3, **DNA is not merely a code of heredity—it is a frequency broadcaster**. Each strand transmits signals to your cells that either resonate with harmony or amplify dissonance. When the body is flooded with toxins, negative emotional charge, or incoherent stimuli, these DNA signals distort, leading to confusion in the body and breakdown in the field.

The pineal, as the body's spiritual antenna, is deeply sensitive to these vibrational states. If DNA is the signal, the pineal is the receiver.

To **decalcify** and restore its function is not just a physical task—it is a form of **spiritual refinement**. It requires clean water, clean food, clean air, and most importantly, **clean thought**.

But there are also tools—natural supports that assist the body in releasing the residue that clouds the signal.

- **Iodine** helps displace fluoride and bromide—two halogens that accumulate in the pineal and disrupt its function.
- **Boron** supports the detoxification of heavy metals and protects neuronal tissue.
- **Raw cacao**, rich in magnesium and antioxidants, increases blood flow to the brain and nourishes the gland.
- **Chlorella** and **spirulina** bind to toxins and help carry them out of the system.
- **Tamarind** has been shown to assist in excreting fluoride.
- **Sunlight**, especially early morning light, helps restore the circadian rhythm and activate pineal function naturally.
- **Earthing**—walking barefoot on natural ground—recalibrates the body's electromagnetic balance.
- **Sound therapy** using frequencies such as **963 Hz** (the so-called God frequency) can help stimulate and resonate the pineal directly.

The pineal gland, in this system, is like the *master receiver*—the spiritual eye that interprets the vibrational tone of the body.

To awaken it is to realign your signal—to bring the whole system back into **harmony with the CORE field**.

The purer the vessel, the more profound the signal.

DETOX BEYOND THE BODY: EMOTIONAL, MENTAL, RELATIONAL, SPIRITUAL

True purification is not limited to what you eat or drink. Detoxing is not just physical—it is emotional, mental, and relational.

Your emotions carry charge. If you suppress them, they compress and become woven into your fabric—and harder to remove. If you indulge them without awareness, they control you. But if you feel them fully and consciously release them, you can master them and **retune the field**.

Unprocessed grief blurs the lens.

Stored anger creates internal friction.

Guilt loops vibrate shame into the signal, and the outcome is a collapse into lower timelines, where rejection, punishment, or self-sabotage reappear as karmic echoes.

These residues don't just sit in your psychology. They live in your frequency. They stain the soul. And they broadcast outward, shaping what you attract, what you see, and what you feel.

Mental detox is just as essential. This means releasing looping thoughts, cynicism, comparison, and internal narratives that bind you to lower states.

It means watching your inner dialogue.

Not every thought deserves a platform.

Not every fear needs a microphone.

In today's world one of the most overlooked forms of toxicity is **what we allow into our minds**.

We are feeding our awareness a steady diet of digital noise—scrolling endlessly through social media, absorbing content laced with fear, comparison, sarcasm, and violence. We consume imagery steeped in war, chaos, and murder, often within seconds of waking up.

And it's not just visual content—**chaotic music** can distort your field just as powerfully.

Much of today's mainstream music is tuned to 440 Hz—a frequency that some researchers argue induces tension and unease, compared with the natural resonance of 432 Hz.

Add in dissonant rhythms, aggressive lyrics, and synthetic production techniques, and what you're listening to is not music—it's vibrational interference.

Just as harmonic tones bring order to cymatic plates, disharmonic sound breaks structure apart. Over time these sonic distortions can leave you energetically fragmented, agitated, or emotionally dulled—without ever realizing the cause.

This is not harmless; it's **vibrational programming**.

Studies have shown a clear link between **increased social media use and higher rates of anxiety, depression, and attention fragmentation**, especially among adolescents and young adults. Your field is constantly collapsing frames based on what you consume. If your inputs are saturated with chaos, your field will reflect it.

But it goes deeper than content. The very devices we use emit **electromagnetic frequencies** that interfere with our biology.

This isn't fringe. Patents filed with the US government detail methods for influencing human physiology using electromagnetic and acoustic frequencies. One such patent describes how **subliminal acoustic pulses** can be used to excite sensory resonances in the nervous system, causing effects such as sleepiness, disorientation, or even emotional shifts without conscious awareness.[18] Another outlines **neuromodulation via electromagnetic fields**, with the capacity to influence the nervous system noninvasively.[19] These technologies suggest what many have long intuited: Frequency is not just a force—it is a control mechanism.

Research on **5G and microwave radiation** has revealed a growing body of evidence pointing to neurological and behavioral effects in lab animals. In controlled studies mice and rats exposed to high-frequency electromagnetic fields, particularly in the 1.5 GHz to 4.9 GHz range, exhibited signs of increased anxiety, impaired memory, and changes in emotional behavior.[54, 55] Exposure to 2650 MHz fields, for example, produced anxiety-like responses, even in the absence of depression or spatial memory loss.[20] At 4.9 GHz, researchers observed depression-like behaviors and disruptions in the amygdala, the brain region associated with emotional regulation.[21] When this RF exposure was combined with electromagnetic pulse events, the neurological impact intensified, with altered neurotransmitter activity and stress-related behavior patterns.[22] Additional experiments at 1.5 GHz and 4.3 GHz frequencies revealed measurable cognitive deficits and physical changes to hippocampal tissue—the area critical for memory and learning.[23]

Books such as *The Invisible Rainbow* by Arthur Firstenberg document the rise of **chronic illness, neurological disturbance, and mood disorders** alongside the expansion of the global electrical grid, from the telegraph to Wi-Fi. This is not coincidence—it is resonance.

We are **electrical beings** living in an **electromagnetic soup**, and few have been taught how to defend, discharge, or detox from it.

It is vibrational pollution.

And it is one of the primary reasons so many live in a state of **chronic disharmony, anxiety, and spiritual confusion.**

Consuming this kind of input is like fueling a high-performance sports car with swamp water. The engine might run but not for long—and certainly not at the level it was designed for. In CR your body is that sports car. Your awareness is the driver. And the content you ingest—through your eyes, ears, thoughts, and relationships—is the fuel.

When you consume distorted signals, you begin to broadcast distorted signals. The field does not distinguish between what you generate and what you ingest—both become part of your vibrational architecture. In CR this is especially dangerous because it draws you out of alignment with the **CORE field**—the baseline harmony of your natural, divine frequency.

As explored in chapter 3, disharmony from the CORE field has physiological implications. When you fall out of resonance with it, your organs, your brain waves, and even your DNA begin to emit irregular patterns. Your very biology can start vibrating in dissonance, contributing to illness, fatigue, and mental fog, not because something is broken but because the signal has been scrambled.

Purifying your mental environment is not about ignoring the world. It is about choosing what you tune to. When you feed your mind positive content—beauty, stillness, truth, compassion—you support its return to a natural frequency. You support healing. You support creation.

Relational detox is perhaps the most overlooked. Every person you allow into your field is part of your vibrational ecosystem. That doesn't mean cutting people off impulsively—it means noticing how your frequency responds in their presence.

Do they lift your tone? Or scatter it?
Do they speak to your higher self? Or drag you into loops?
Love everyone. But curate your inner circle.

It is vibrational hygiene.

PURIFICATION IS NOT MORAL—IT IS VIBRATIONAL INTEGRITY

We live in a culture where detox is often equated with virtue. But purification is not about being "good." It is about being clear.

This distinction matters deeply.

Vibrational purity is not about purity in the religious or perfectionist sense. It is about energetic alignment. To purify is to remove the dissonance that clouds your natural harmonious tone.

You are not adding something new.
You are removing the interference that blocks what you already are.

This is why judgment has no place in this work. You are not purifying to earn worthiness. There is no superiority—treat everyone with respect. You are purifying because your field wants to sing.

THE ILLUSION OF SUCCESS WITHOUT ALIGNMENT

It is true that some people live in deep incoherence—and still manifest material success. They may be manipulative, dishonest, or selfish. Yet they appear to "win."

In material terms they may appear untouchable. Wealth, power, influence. Their tone—though distorted—is focused and strong. And the field, being vibrationally neutral, responds to that frequency.

A person can maintain vibrational coherence—clarity of signal—without ethical alignment. If their beliefs, emotions, and intentions are unified (even around distorted aims), they will collapse frames that reflect that tone.

This explains why some "bad people" get good results. Coherence still works because the field responds to frequency, not morality.

But here is the deeper truth: Coherence without love is unstable. It may manifest short-term success, but it lacks sustainability. It creates karmic recoil. It collapses frames that feed the ego but poison the soul.

Eventually the tone becomes unbearable. The field collapses inward. And the incoherence reveals itself.

True success—the kind that brings peace, joy, clarity, and growth—only comes when coherence is paired with integrity, love, and compassion.

It's easy to lash out, to snap, to collapse into lower frames when triggered. These reactions often feel automatic. But in truth they are learned loops—vibrational habits. The real power is in the pause. In the space between stimulus and response. That's where frequency is chosen, not inherited.

LIVING IN DISHARMONY: COLLAPSING DISTORTED FRAMES

When your field is out of sync—when your body is burdened, your emotions are turbulent, your mind is chaotic—you begin collapsing distorted frames.

Life feels off. Things don't flow. You're met with resistance, confusion, miscommunication. You may call it bad luck or stress, but it is simply feedback, reverberations of your disharmony from the CORE field.

Your field is speaking to you through your experiences.
The distortion outside is the echo of disharmony inside.

Purification leads to liberation. The more you detox your body, emotions, mind, and relationships, the more clearly you broadcast your soul's harmonious tone.

And when that tone becomes clean, coherent, and consistent, you begin collapsing frames that feel like truth. Like ease. Like grace.

This is the resonance of **gamma**—the brain's highest frequency of coherence and integration. In gamma your field synchronizes across all layers—mind, body, heart, and soul. The frame you collapse from that state is not forced. It unfolds with elegant precision. You don't manifest from desperation—you emanate from alignment, not because you're striving but because you're aligned.

Not all purification arrives gently. Sometimes it comes as sorrow, grief, guilt, or obstacles.

Compression before expansion.

Just as a breath requires contraction before the inhale, or sound waves narrow before releasing their full amplitude, your field often tightens before it opens. These periods of inner pressure—often experienced as hardship, confusion, or emotional intensity—are not signs that you've lost your way. They are signals that your system is preparing for expansion if you meet it with the right frequency.

Compression is not failure. It is feedback. It is the field bracing for transformation. Something within you is being dislodged—old frequencies, outdated patterns, false identities—and the clearing may feel like chaos before it reveals the reward.

These are not interruptions in your journey. They are initiations.

Mistakes become teachers.

Pain reveals where the tone is out of tune.

Loss reminds us of what truly mattered beneath what we thought we wanted.

This is not to romanticize suffering but to reframe it as an intelligent, if often unwanted, phase of refinement.

You are not being punished. You are being tuned.

A powerful practice in CR is to revisit your own past. Write down the major moments of hardship in your life—losses, betrayals, illnesses, failures—and next to each, reflect honestly.

What did this experience teach me? What kind of strength or awareness did it call forward in me that I didn't know I had?

When viewed this way, even painful chapters reveal themselves as inflection points—moments when your field was being recalibrated for a more coherent future.

It is through pain and disruption that we often grow the most because suffering shakes loose what comfort would never confront. Our greatest leaps in awareness rarely come through ease but through the frequencies we're forced to face and finally transmute.

Still, this must be held with tenderness. Not all suffering is equal. Some people carry trauma that is profound, unchosen, and unjust. CR does not ask anyone to glorify their pain or ignore their grief. But it does offer this: If the CORE field is always seeking coherence, then even the most difficult seasons may hold an opportunity, not to be erased or forgotten but to be reclaimed, conquered, and transmuted into wisdom.

You can ask, *What if this is here to reveal who I really am? What can I learn from this experience?*

Sometimes the answers come years later.

You grow not despite the compression but often because of it. Like a seed buried beneath the soil, the pressure cracks you open so that you can grow out of the darkness and reach the light.

To raise your frequency is not just to ascend. It is to lighten the field so that it can carry more light. And with every step you take toward clarity, you don't just elevate your own timeline. You elevate the field for everyone connected to you.

As explored in chapter 5, you are not a closed system. You carry echoes of your ancestors—unresolved grief, inherited fears, looping patterns. When you heal, you shift more than just your own field.

You release **karmic momentum**.
You break **fractal recurrence**.
And in doing so, you open a new timeline, not only for yourself but also for those who came before and those who will follow.

You become a mirror of possibility.
A tuning fork for peace.
A walking signal of coherence.

And in that tone—pure, strong, simple—the universe begins to respond.

SPIRITUAL CLEANSING—REMOVING THE STATIC OF FEAR

Before renewal can take hold, the field must be cleared. And at the root of most distortion is **fear**.

Fear is not just an emotion—it is a contraction of the field.

It narrows perception, accelerates brain waves, and scrambles the signal. In fear you collapse defensive frames. You enter survival timelines. Your decisions become reactive, not resonant. This is why spiritual traditions across cultures emphasize **cleansing**—not just of body but of soul. Whether through confession, fasting, ritual washing, or silent prayer, the intention is the same: to release what distorts and return to what is real.

In CR **spiritual cleansing is vibrational decluttering**.

It means releasing the tones of fear, guilt, resentment, and shame.

It means naming them, feeling them fully, and then allowing them to move.

Because when fear is transmuted, the CORE field flows freely again.

Here's a simple practice:

- Sit in silence.
- Breathe into the heart.
- Name the fear aloud.
- Say gently, "I release this tone. I return to coherence."

TRUTHFULNESS—THE COHERENCE OF EXPRESSION

One of the deepest forms of spiritual cleansing is learning not to lie.

Lies are not just moral issues—they are *vibrational misalignments*. To lie is to speak one frequency while holding another. This dissonance fractures the field. It requires energy to maintain, and it embeds subtle incoherence into the moment you're shaping.

In CR truthfulness is coherence between thought, word, and tone.

It doesn't mean brutal honesty or performative transparency. It means your **inner state matches your outer expression**. That your waveform is clean. Clear. Aligned.

Every time you lie—even in small ways, even white lies—you introduce static into your resonance. You split your awareness. You weaken the power of your own word.

But when you speak truth, even when it's hard,

- your field strengthens,
- your awareness stabilizes, and
- your ability to collapse reality into clarity sharpens.

THE HEART: PORTAL TO HARMONY

The heart is a central organ of perception—a portal through which harmony, coherence, and creation are made possible.

The heart generates the most powerful electromagnetic field in the human body. Its electrical field, as measured by an electrocardiogram, is about sixty times greater in amplitude than the brain's electrical activity recorded in an EEG.[24] Moreover, the magnetic component of the heart's field is approximately one hundred times stronger than that produced by the brain. This magnetic field can be detected several feet away from the body using sensitive magnetometers, such as Superconducting Quantum Interference Devices (SQUID).[25] Importantly, this field is dynamic and reflects our emotional states, changing in response to feelings such as love, compassion, or anger. These fluctuations suggest that the heart's electromagnetic field plays a role in internal regulation and may influence the external environment.

When you feel love, compassion, or gratitude, your heart rhythm becomes smooth, sine-like, and balanced. It entrains the brain, synchronizes the nervous system, and creates a harmonized signal that can stabilize the entire field. You literally begin broadcasting a frequency that pulls other systems—internal and external—into resonance with it.

This is why in CR, coherence begins in the heart—it is how we raise our level of awareness. The rhythm of the heart becomes the rhythm of the field. And the rhythm of the field becomes the architecture of your experience.

HOLDING THE BREATH—ENTERING STILLNESS, CLEARING INTERFERENCE

One of the most profound demonstrations of the heart's power is what happens in moments of stillness, specifically in the space between breaths.

When you gently hold the breath after an exhale, not forcefully but with relaxed presence, something remarkable occurs. The body becomes silent. The breath is still. And in that pause, all muscular and mental interference drops away.

What remains is the pulse.
The beat of the heart.

In that moment the heart becomes the only signal. Its rhythm is no longer competing with erratic breath or scattered thought. It stands alone, pure and clear.

This clarity is not just felt energetically—it's measurable physiologically. During normal breathing, blood flow from the legs back to the heart can create subtle fluctuations in heart rate and internal pressure. These oscillations add **noise to the signal**—tiny disruptions that affect the nervous system and brain's ability to synchronize.

But when the breath is held after exhale, these mechanical fluctuations diminish. Circulatory flow slows. Muscular engagement ceases. The autonomic nervous system quiets, and heart rate variability becomes more stable. Studies have shown that **brief breath holds** improve baroreflex sensitivity—a key marker of heart-brain coherence—and increase parasympathetic tone, allowing the body to drop into deep regulation and awareness.[26, 27]

In other words **stillness isn't passive—it is a precision tool for vibrational alignment**.

Holding the breath gently allows the heart to speak without interference.

It reveals that the heart is not simply keeping you alive. It is tuning you, moment by moment. It is offering a consistent waveform—a vibrational foundation upon which everything else is built.

Practicing this kind of heart-focused breath hold even for a few seconds a day can attune your awareness to the quiet strength of your inner field. It reminds you that coherence is always one breath—and one beat—away.

LOVE, GRATITUDE, AND REVERENCE–TONAL TUNERS

Specific emotional states have a unique ability to tune the heart field—and, by extension, your entire being. Among them, three stand out in CR's vibrational model: love, gratitude, and reverence.

These states are not just pleasant feelings. They are frequencies. And when consciously cultivated, they bring the heart into its optimal pattern—smooth, wide, and harmonically balanced.

Love opens the field. It dissolves resistance. It softens contraction and invites unity with others and the moment.

Gratitude centers the field. It grounds your awareness in abundance, reminding your system that all is already given.

Reverence elevates the field. It connects you to something greater than yourself—God, Source, the CORE field—and lifts your tone to match that higher presence.

Practicing these frequencies is not about forcing emotion. It is about tuning attention.

You can feel reverence by looking at a sunrise.

You can feel gratitude by breathing into your lungs.

You can feel love by simply placing your hand on your chest and remembering that you are alive.

These are not abstract sentiments. They are tuning mechanisms.

When activated, they bring your field into harmony. And when your field harmonizes, the moment harmonizes with it.

THE HEART AS ARCHITECT OF HARMONY

The CR model makes a bold but essential claim: The heart is not the seat of emotion—it is the architect of harmony.

This means your ability to stabilize reality, collapse frames cleanly, and live in resonance does not begin in the intellect. It begins in the chest.

We are taught to solve problems with the mind. To analyze, argue, calculate, and control. But when the mind is not aligned with the heart, its intelligence becomes sterile. It fractures rather than unifies. It collapses partial truths instead of coherent realities.

But when the heart leads—when the mind serves the tone of the heart—something shifts. Clarity emerges. Timing synchronizes. Perception expands. You no longer force reality into shape. You allow the tone of coherence to shape it for you.

This is the essence of CR's vibrational metaphysics:
The field organizes around tone.
Tone is set by coherence.
And coherence begins in the heart.

REDEMPTION AND RENEWAL BEGIN IN THE HEART

You cannot think your way into a new timeline.
You must tune your way in.

And that tuning begins with the heart.

Redemption—the return to right alignment—does not start with new ideas. It starts with new resonance. The moment you soften, forgive, and allow your heart to open again, the field begins to shift. You send out a new tone. And that tone begins drawing in new frames.

In spiritual language this is the moment of repentance, the return to grace. This is acknowledging your wrongdoings, taking accountability, and asking for forgiveness. In CR it is vibrational reset. Either way the path is the same: The heart must turn before the world can.

Renewal, too, begins in the heart. You might not see the effects immediately. But once the signal has changed, the new frame is already collapsing. You have already stepped into the future you were waiting for.

The heart is not soft.
It is strong.

You don't just find peace for yourself.
You broadcast it.

And in doing so, you don't just change your life.
You change the field around you.
You become a resonance that others can feel, attune to, and remember.

This is how coherence spreads:
One heart.
One tone.
One silent beat at a time.

LIVING AS A COHERENT CREATOR

Life is not a linear string of disconnected events. It only appears that way when viewed through the lens of fragmented awareness. In truth life is vibrationally ordered. Each moment is not isolated but harmonic. It carries the resonance of what came before and seeds the conditions for what comes next.

We should not view reality as something external happening to you. It is something emanating *from* you. Each frame of your experience arises in response to your frequency—your thoughts, your emotions, your breath, your tone. And because of this, your life is better understood not as a timeline but as a *waveform*.

You are always shaping time, even when you don't realize it. You are either collapsing reality by default—through unconscious habits, reactive thoughts, and inherited frequencies—or you are collapsing it by design—through intentional coherence, awareness, and vibrational alignment.

A movement from passive experiencer to active creator. From accidental collapse to conscious authorship.

When your inner world is disorganized, time feels chaotic. Events appear random. Life becomes difficult to navigate. You may feel like things happen *to* you, with no pattern or purpose. But this confusion is not punishment. It is feedback. It is the echo of a scattered field trying to stabilize itself.

On the other hand, when your field becomes coherent—when your intention, emotion, body, and spirit align—the external world begins to shift. Time opens up. Space feels softer. People respond differently. Opportunities seem to arrive with less effort. Life begins to synchronize, not because you're trying to control it but because your tone is clean.

This is what it means to live as a coherent creator.

You no longer chase outcomes. You tune your signal. You refine your state. You trust that your field is intelligent enough to bring you exactly what matches your frequency. You become less concerned with controlling the future and more devoted to collapsing the present moment with care.

Self-mastery, in this light, is not about suppressing your impulses or perfecting your behavior. It is about frequency stewardship. It is the art of tending to your tone the way a musician cares for their instrument. As we described in chapter 3, you begin to notice how your words and thoughts carry resonance. How your emotional patterns become broadcast loops. How even a single internal shift can alter the quality of the moments that follow.

You take ownership, not out of guilt but out of *power*.

And with that power comes peace.

This is how time expands, not because the seconds stretch but because your awareness deepens. You begin to experience more of each frame. You become present to the fullness of now. You move through life with less reactivity and more rhythm.

You may still face challenges. You may still encounter loss, conflict, or uncertainty. But you will meet them as a coherent field, not as a scattered one. You will move through them without collapsing into them.

And this changes everything.
It means you can choose your tone before your circumstances change.
It means you can bring peace to a room, not just absorb its tension.
It means you can live on purpose, not just by inertia.

Let this be your path forward:
Tend to your frequency with devotion.
Speak only what you wish to manifest.
Feel only what you are willing to amplify.
And collapse each frame as if it were sacred—because it is.

Coherence is not meant to be hoarded.

When you carry a clear tone into your relationships, you begin to entrain the fields around you.

A single coherent person can shift a room. A group of them can shift a culture.

In this way your coherence is not private; it is contagious.

You become a stabilizer amid the chaos. A mirror for what is possible.

This is not a call to fix others.

It is an invitation to fix your own frequency to become so harmonized that others remember their own original tone just by being near you. In the CORE field, coherence is communal. When we rise together, reality doesn't just bend. It sings.

LOVE: THE LANGUAGE OF THE CORE FIELD

At the center of CR is not just a theory of vibration or a model of consciousness—it is a return to the CORE field. And at the center of the CORE field is a single, undeniable truth: **Love is its language.**

Love is not merely a feeling. It is the original resonance. The master tone. The native frequency of the field from which all form arises. When your awareness finds harmony with the CORE, what you feel is not abstraction—it is love. It is warmth, clarity, safety, connection, and expansion all at once.

Every spiritual tradition, at its core, has pointed to this. The Bible says "God is love" (1 John 4:8, New King James Version). Not *has* love. *Is* love. Love is the medium of divine communication. The waveform of creation. The frequency that organizes light, matter, time, and space into harmony.

This is why love heals. Why it transforms. Why it stretches time and softens the moment. Not because of what it does but because of what it *is*. Love brings you back into alignment with the organizing pattern of the universe itself.

When you feel love—true, coherent love—you are no longer separate from God. You are no longer guessing your way through the dark. You are tuned, not just emotionally but metaphysically. You begin to speak the language the field understands.

Those who reach the highest states of **gamma coherence**—whether through deep meditation, near-death experiences, breathwork, or moments of profound spiritual insight—report the same thing: not just heightened awareness but **unconditional love**.

In gamma the brain enters full-spectrum synchrony. But the heart enters **oneness**.

The sense of separation dissolves. Time slows. Judgment vanishes.

What remains is **pure, resonant presence** and the unmistakable feeling of being held by something infinite. In the highest frequencies of awareness, love is not something you feel—it is what you become. And from that place, **every breath, every word, every choice becomes a transmission**.

This is why the practices described throughout this chapter—breath, silence, intention, sound, and coherence—are not ends in themselves. They are portals. They are ways of clearing enough interference so that love can be felt again, heard again, broadcast again.

But love is more than a state you feel. Love is also the frequency through which *reality responds*. When you enter a room in a state of love, the field shifts. The people within it soften. Events rearrange themselves. You do not have to say a word. Your field speaks first.

And when you collapse a moment in love—when you speak through it, breathe through it, move through it—that moment becomes fertile ground. New frames unfold. Healing becomes possible.

Time expands. The heart opens. The field aligns.

The field responds to tone. And love is the purest tone of all.

This also explains why fear and shame collapse jagged realities. They are not "bad" in a moral sense—they are *out of phase* with the CORE. They carry fragmentation. They introduce distortion into the field.

And in doing so, they create feedback that feels chaotic, unstable, or painful.

Love, by contrast, stabilizes.
It harmonizes.
It builds coherence from the inside out.

You cannot fake love. You cannot manufacture it through force. But you can remove what blocks it. You can sit in silence. You can breathe gently. You can remember someone who loves you, or something you are grateful for, or a time when you felt truly seen.

And from there the signal returns.
You feel it in your chest.
You feel it in your breath.
You feel it in the way the moment softens.
You feel it in the way your body says, "Yes. This is it."
Love is not the reward.
It is the origin.

And when your field is aligned with it, you are not just more spiritual. You are more *you.*

This is the highest form of coherence: when you become a consistent transmitter of love.

This is why, for example, Jesus is so often depicted with His heart exposed, glowing, radiant, and open. It is not a metaphor. It is a message. His sacred heart is the highest vibrational expression of divine love made manifest in human form. He is the embodiment of the CORE field in flesh and blood.

His life was not only a lesson in compassion but also a frequency transmission. Everything he did—his mercy, his truth, his sacrifice—

emitted a tone of love so pure it reorganized the world. And the rever-berations are still felt today.

When you tune to love, you are not just aligning with an abstract field.

You are entering resonance with the CORE field—the tone through which all things were made.

Close your eyes.
Place your hand over your heart.
Breathe slowly.
And remember:
You are not just a passenger in this life.
You are a composer of frames.
A steward of frequency.
A vessel of the divine.
Let your breath be rhythmic.
Let your tone be clear.
Let your field be love.
And from that love, let the world unfold.

You are not just shaping the next moment.
You are shaping your relationship to time itself.
Because as your field becomes coherent—clean, stable, aligned—your awareness begins to stretch.
Not just through space but through *frames*.
This is the threshold of eternity.

In the next chapter, we explore what happens when awareness be-comes so tuned, so present that time bends open.

We enter the infinite now, not as concept but as lived experience.
    Where déjà vu, synchronicity, and mystical union are not

anomalies but natural signs that your field has become transparent to the timeless.

Coherence leads to collapse.

Collapse leads to stillness.

And stillness . . . becomes the doorway.

7

THE THRESHOLD
OF ETERNITY

*When a thought of Plato becomes a thought to me—when a truth
that fired the soul of a Hebrew prophet fires mine—time is no more.*
—RALPH WALDO EMERSON

THE I AM AND THE TIMELESS NOW

The Saturn crew had become familiar with silence. But this
time it wasn't the vacuum of space they were hearing—it was
something deeper. It was the sound of no longer searching.
No longer striving. No longer narrating. Something within them had
stilled.

Outside their ship Earth turned slowly beneath a blanket of stars.
Yet inside time had begun to dissolve. There were no clocks in their
minds, no next tasks, no lingering thoughts of home or mission.
Instead, there was only now. And that now had become so expansive, so complete that it no longer felt like a moment at all. It felt like
eternity.

This threshold is what we call the I AM or gamma. It is a vibrational state—a pure form of awareness that exists before identity, before story, before time. It is the unfiltered witness that remains when the noise, body, and ego fall away. It is the stable field of being beneath all doing.

Some meditative and psychedelic states report an even finer level of awareness—one in which not only time and ego dissolve, but even the sense of observation itself softens into pure being. These ultrarefined states have been correlated with brain wave frequencies above 100 Hz, sometimes reaching into the 200–600 Hz range, a band some researchers refer to as **lambda.**

This frequency is difficult to measure with standard EEGs, but studies on advanced Tibetan meditators and cross-frequency coherence in deep absorption states suggest its presence during the most profound mystical experiences.

Despite these tantalizing signals, **lambda remains one of the least researched and least understood territories in neurophenomenology.** *There is a conspicuous absence of peer-reviewed, high-resolution studies that consistently capture or validate this band.*

The tools of mainstream neuroscience were not built to track the rarefied terrain of consciousness that lambda points to. What little we do know comes largely from fringe studies, oral traditions, and anecdotal reports from seasoned contemplatives. This epistemic gap is not a discredit but a challenge: **Lambda sits just beyond the edge of scientific instrumentation, much like early quantum effects once lay beyond classical physics.** The silence around it may reflect not insignificance but subtlety.

In lambda the mind doesn't merely observe unity—it becomes indistinguishable from it. Identity evaporates, and what remains is a seamless field of awareness—what mystics might call Source, God, or the void that vibrates with life. This is not imagination or metaphor. It's the neural signature of total surrender, where frequency becomes field, and the observer merges with the CORE.

CR views lambda not as an achievement but as a dimensional re-membering—the vibrational threshold where eternity stops being visited and starts being lived. And yet even this transcendent state—the lambda field—is not the final destination. It is a gateway back to something more intimate, more original: the I AM.

The I AM is not something we create. It is something that was created. Something we remember. It is the part of us that has never been frag-mented, even when every other part was scattered. It is the original tone—the one we carried before we were named, before we were con-ditioned, before we were shaped by the filmstrip of experience. The part of us that always lives in the CORE field. It is the one inside that watches and waits, eagerly anticipating the day we return to harmony.

Across mystical traditions, this state has been described with many names. In Christianity it is the stillness in which one hears the "still small voice" of God. In Eastern thought, it is the ground of being—Brahman, the Tao, or the witness self. In contemplative prayer it is the surrender of all thought until only awareness remains. In each case the description points to the same experience: a state in which there is no longer a distinction between the observer and the ob-served. There is only presence—a merger with the CORE field.

These moments come with no fanfare, no external confirmation, and often no words. They are not Instagrammable. There is no one else there to congratulate you. But when they arise, something unmis-takable is felt: a kind of radiant stillness. A peace that cannot be ex-plained. A gentle yet absolute clarity that you are not your thoughts, not your story, not your timeline. You simply are.

As Walt Whitman wrote, "I exist as I am, that is enough. If no other in the world be aware, I sit content. And if each and all be aware, I sit content."

This is not just a psychological shift but as a vibrational one. When you enter the I AM, your awareness ceases to collapse frames reactively. You are no longer oscillating between past and future. You are no longer creating from fragmented beliefs. Your tone becomes singular. Your field becomes whole. And with that wholeness, the illusion of time loses its grip.

Presence, then, is not a mental exercise. It is not about "living in the moment" as a strategy for better productivity or peace of mind. It is the natural consequence of gamma coherence. When your field becomes stable—when your breath, thoughts, and emotions align—the structure of time begins to dissolve. Not in the sense that events stop happening but in the sense that your consciousness stops organizing itself around them. You are no longer tethered to a sequence. You are centered in the source.

This is why the present moment holds such spiritual power. It is not just a moment in time. It is the place where all time becomes transparent. The now is not a tiny sliver between the past and future—it is the doorway through which eternity is accessed. When you are anchored in the now, you are standing at the intersection of all possibility. And in that stillness, the I AM becomes active.

The Saturn crew had not discovered anything new. What they found had been there all along. But it was only in the silence—only in the total coherence of their awareness—that they became able to hear it. And what they heard was not a message. It was a presence. It was the memory of what had always been true.

TIMELESSNESS IN PRACTICE: CASE STUDIES AND STATES OF FLOW

Timelessness is not an abstraction. It is something many people have felt—if only for a moment. And while language often struggles to capture it, the experience is unmistakable: Time seems to pause, stretch, or disappear entirely. The boundaries between self and action dissolve. What remains is pure presence—expansive, fluid, and deeply coherent.

Artists know this state. Athletes know it. So do monks, mystics, and ordinary people caught in extraordinary moments of awareness.

Consider the painter who loses track of the afternoon as brush and breath move in perfect rhythm. Or the athlete who suddenly sees the entire field in slow motion, their body responding before thought arrives. Or the musician midperformance who finds themselves being played by the music rather than the other way around.

These are flow states—moments when awareness and activity become seamless. Neuroscience shows that during such states, brain wave patterns often shift toward greater coherence. Disparate regions of the brain begin to fire in synchrony. The sense of time as a ticking clock fades. And in its place arises a deeper rhythm—one that matches the task, the body, and the field in perfect harmony.[1, 2, 3]

Near-death experiences often include similar reports. People who have crossed the threshold of death and returned speak of life reviews that unfold in an instant or encounters with realms where time has no meaning. Some describe the sensation of "always now"—a boundless moment in which all events seem to coexist. What's striking is that many near-death experiences include a profound sense of peace, clarity, and unconditional love.

Meditators, too, frequently describe timeless states. In the quiet of sustained attention, the mind slows and thoughts thin. Eventually, thought itself may dissolve, not into nothingness but into presence. In this space, minutes can feel like hours or disappear altogether. There is no striving, no measurement—just being. The "I" that is usually tethered to a timeline softens, and what remains is awareness itself—calm, boundless, awake.

Across these examples—flow, death, and meditation—the common thread is not technique, environment, or belief. It is **heightened awareness and internal coherence**. The body is relaxed. The mind is clear. Emotion is steady. And the field becomes whole.

In the most profound of these states—whether brought on by near-death experiences, deep meditation, or psychedelics—something remarkable can occur: **ego death**.

Ego death is not annihilation. It is **dis-identification** from the body and self—the construct made of stories, labels, fears, and memories. When the field becomes fully coherent, when awareness stabilizes without grasping, the personal identity that once felt central begins to dissolve. There is no longer a "me" moving through time—there is only presence, unfolding from within.

This dissolution can feel terrifying to the unprepared ego. It resists its own unraveling. But once released, what emerges is not void—it is vastness. Still. Alive. Aware. The observer remains but untethered to narrative. Free of compression.

Ego death is the moment when awareness no longer filters or collapses reality through identity.

The waveform of "I" becomes spacious, fluid, continuous.

And in that state, a paradox is revealed:

You have not disappeared. You have returned.

To what you were before the story began.

Timelessness is the natural outcome of vibrational integrity. When your awareness is aligned and your field is cleansed, time ceases to push against you. It becomes spacious. Elastic. Transparent.

But it is important to recognize that most of these peak experiences are temporary. Athletes, artists, and near-death experiencers often stumble into gamma-like coherence by accident or extremity—*a brush with death, a burst of inspiration, a perfect game.* These moments are glimpses. Portals.

The practices described in chapter 6—cleansing the field, raising frequency, stabilizing breath and thought—are how you make such moments **sustainable**. They are how you *earn* access to coherence not just in performance but in daily life.

Where flow states are lightning, **chapter 6 is the grounding rod**. It shows you how to become a conductor for timelessness—by clearing what distorts and strengthening what aligns.

And the more often you practice daily, the more natural this state becomes.

Timelessness is not a gift for the few.
It is our collective native language.

THE POWER OF STILLNESS
In stillness there is power.

Not the kind of power the world usually seeks—not domination, speed, or control—but something much deeper. Something subtler. In stillness there is access. There is clarity. There is the quiet reorganization of the soul. Stillness is not the absence of movement—it is the *alignment of frequency*.

Stillness is often misunderstood. In a culture that glorifies productivity, stimulus, and distraction, stillness is treated as idleness, as wasted potential. But true stillness is not passivity. It is precision. It is the moment when the scattered fragments of your awareness rejoin into one clean tone. And when this tone harmonizes with the CORE field, something extraordinary happens: The frame opens.

You begin to *see* the architecture behind the moment. You feel the scaffolding of reality—the subtle structures holding experience in place. In stillness you don't just observe time. You observe the patterning beneath it. You see how your tone shapes the field, how your breath carries your awareness, how even your thoughts are sculpting the frames you are about to walk into. You find meaning, and emotion rolls away. You find purpose.

Sometimes, in this stillness, you catch glimpses—flashes of memory you cannot place, dreams that feel more real than waking life, or moments of déjà vu that ripple with familiarity. These are not illusions. They are moments of frame overlap—where your awareness briefly brushes against a parallel timeline, an alternate life, or a nested layer of self.

Timeless awareness includes access to more than the present. It opens the window to the structure of reality—where multiple timelines coexist, where soul paths spiral and intersect, and where memory, intuition, and knowing are not bound by linear cause and effect.

These glimpses are invitations. To recognize that your consciousness is far more expansive than the live story you are currently living. In stillness the moment becomes transparent enough to reveal these echoes, and in that revelation, your sense of self begins to stretch beyond a single lifetime, a single storyline, or a single identity.

Stillness is the natural consequence of gamma coherence. When your brain waves synchronize across wide regions, when your heart rhythm becomes sine-like and harmonic, and when your nervous system enters balance, your awareness stabilizes. The internal chatter quiets. The mind stops chasing and defending. And instead, you enter presence. Spacious, luminous, and awake.

In this state, time no longer feels linear. It begins to stretch. A minute may feel eternal. A thought may carry a thousand realizations. You are not asleep. You are more awake than ever, but your awareness is no longer confined by materialism and ticking seconds. It hovers just above time's surface, moving not by measure but by depth.

Stillness is the doorway to eternity. And yet it is always available. It does not require withdrawal from the world. It does not require wealth or privilege. It only requires you—*in your simplest form.* The form you entered this Earth with.

This is why mystics across traditions have emphasized silence, not as escape but as return. When Jesus withdrew to pray, when Buddha sat beneath the bodhi tree, and when the prophets retreated to mountaintops, it was not to abandon life but to *reenter* it through stillness. They were not running from the world. They were tuning their field so they could move through it with clarity.

Stillness reveals things that noise cannot. It reveals truth. It reveals the next step without effort. It reveals the signal you've been carrying all along but couldn't hear until the interference subsided.

And perhaps most importantly, stillness reveals God—stillness is where you meet the CORE without distortion. It is where you stop broadcasting survival signals and begin receiving eternal ones. In that quiet the field speaks. It does not shout. It vibrates.

This is the paradox of spiritual power: It arrives not through striving but through *surrender.*

You do not become powerful by doing more—you become powerful by letting go emotion, fear, and anxiety to *align more precisely*. And stillness is the setting where that alignment becomes possible.

It is where the fragments reunite. Where the past releases. Where the future stops pulling. Where you sit at the center of all time, not moving forward but radiating outward.

And when you learn to enter it by practicing the elements in chapter 6, not occasionally but rhythmically, you unlock your full potential.

Because in that state, you are no longer fragmented. You are tuned. Integrated. Resonating at the frequency of the CORE.

This is where Tesla received downloads—entire blueprints from beyond the veil.

This is where Einstein bent the axis of time and rode thought into the structure of the universe.

EMPATHY, INTEGRITY, AND THE SOUL'S NAVIGATION SYSTEM

Empathy is recognized as a *form of supreme vibrational intelligence*—the ability to enter another person's field without losing the integrity of your own. It is the soul's natural way of navigating shared reality: not through judgment but through compassion. Empathy is a superpower—an instrument of perception so refined that it allows you to *feel* truth in others while remaining rooted in the truth of yourself.

To empathize is to momentarily collapse frames through another's perspective. But true empathy does not mean absorption. It does not mean becoming overwhelmed or losing your center. In its mature form, empathy is gamma in motion. It is the ability to touch another's frequency while continuing to transmit your own. You do not become their pain—you hold space for it without distortion. You do not become their story—you remain the witness who can understand clearly, love deeply, and return home to your own tone.

This balance is rare. Many confuse empathy with enmeshment. They enter the emotional fields of others but fail to stay grounded. They adopt feelings that are not theirs, collapse frames that are not clean, and slowly lose access to their own guidance. In CR this is not empathy—it is incoherence. The field becomes cluttered. Direction becomes confused. And time itself begins to feel distorted.

Worse still, many have been taught that empathy is a weakness—a soft trait to be hardened out of us in favor of logic, detachment, or control. But this is a profound misunderstanding.

Empathy is not fragility. It is frequency literacy.

It is the ability to feel without drowning, to sense without collapsing. When anchored in coherence, empathy becomes a superpower—a tuning fork that lets you read the field without losing your signal.

Gamma coherence is a prerequisite for true empathy. Only when your field is clean can you step into another's without absorbing their static. Only when your awareness is stable can you help another find stillness in their storm.

Empathy is sacred. Because at its highest level, empathy is not about comfort—it is about *communion*. It is the recognition that we are all part of the same field and that to understand another is to briefly harmonize with the music of their soul. There is no purer way to connect to one another.

And how do you know when you're on the right track?

Happiness.

But what is happiness, really? In a world oversaturated with stimuli—notifications, short-form content, instant purchases, and algorithmic pleasures—many people have lost touch with the deeper signal of joy. We confuse distraction for delight. We chase dopamine hits and call it fulfillment. But pleasure and happiness are not the same frequency. One flickers. The other sustains.

Science is beginning to catch up to this truth. Studies in *positive psychology*—from researchers such as Martin Seligman and Mihaly Csikszentmihalyi—show that the most enduring forms of happiness are tied to meaning, connection, gratitude, and flow.[4, 5] These are internal states of coherence, not external achievements. They emerge when the nervous system is calm, when the field is unified, and when the mind and heart speak the same language.

Even entire nations have begun to recognize that GDP is not the true measure of human well-being. In 1972 Bhutan famously introduced the concept of *Gross National Happiness*—a framework that prioritizes psychological well-being, environmental preservation, and cultural integrity over economic output.[6] This reflects a shift from material frequency to spiritual coherence. It suggests that a society's timeline is healthiest not when it produces the most but when it is happiest.

And yet in modern life many people no longer know what truly makes them happy. The signal is buried beneath noise. The compass needle is spinning. Without practices of presence, stillness, and coherence, it becomes difficult to distinguish between fleeting stimulation and soul-level fulfillment. This is why the CR path emphasizes purification, not to restrict pleasure but to rediscover joy. Not to retreat from life but to tune to what is actually life-giving.

To find happiness, begin by subtracting.

Subtract the noise. Subtract the habits that leave you drained. Subtract the beliefs that make you feel small. Subtract the objects and material things. Subtract those in your circle that do not uplift you.

What remains will begin to point the way.

Then listen.

Happiness speaks softly. It's not the loudest voice—it's the most constant. It's the feeling that lingers after the moment ends.

Not pleasure. Not distraction. But the kind of quiet, sustained happiness that arises from inner clarity. Happiness is a *compass.* It tells you when your tone is clean, when your frequency is aligned, and when your actions, thoughts, and beliefs are harmonizing into a single signal. It is how your I AM whispers yes to your direction.

This is why happiness cannot be faked. When it is genuine, it flows through the entire field—physical, mental, emotional, and spiritual. It stretches time. It amplifies coherence. It aligns you with the frames that are meant for you. If something repeatedly steals your happiness, not just your pleasure but your *peace*—it is likely not in resonance with your deeper truth.

And what supports happiness more than anything else?

Integrity.

Integrity means that your thoughts do not betray your heart. That your emotions do not contradict your actions. That your words reflect your beliefs, and your beliefs reflect your soul. When integrity is present, your timeline becomes clear. Your field becomes strong. And time perception itself begins to sharpen.

When your mental, emotional, and spiritual signals align, your awareness expands. You can see more clearly into the past without becoming trapped in it. You can feel more deeply into the present without becoming overwhelmed by it. You can move into the future with confidence, not confusion. Integrity is what stabilizes your navigation system. It gives your compass a true north.

This is why Emerson wrote, "Nothing is at last sacred but the integrity of your own mind." He wasn't calling for stubbornness. He was pointing to coherence. He understood that the sacred is not something distant or esoteric. It is the alignment of thought, spirit, and tone within a single, honest human being.

To live with empathy and integrity is not to be perfect. It is to be *attuned*. And when your tuning is clean, the soul becomes navigable. Life becomes less about searching and more about *remembering*. Less about striving and more about *resonating* with what has always been waiting for you.

Empathy is how we feel one another.

Integrity is how we feel ourselves.

Together they become the soul's true navigation system, guiding us through time not as wanderers but as harmonic beings, returning again and again to coherence.

LIVING DELIBERATELY IN THE ETERNAL FRAME

I wished to live deliberately, to front only the essential facts of life, and see if I could not learn what it had to teach . . .
—HENRY DAVID THOREAU

Thoreau's words were not just about minimalism or retreating into nature—they were about collapsing time *on purpose*. To live deliberately is to collapse each frame with intention. It is to step out of the inertia of unconscious motion and begin engaging each moment as a sculptor. Deliberate living is not about perfection or rigidity. It is about awareness. Precision. Care.

Most people don't live deliberately. They drift. They react. They live on autopilot. They wake up and repeat the same tones, the same thought loops, the same emotional broadcasts, and wonder why nothing changes. They collapse frames by default, not design. And the frames they collapse carry the frequency of confusion, fragmentation, and emotional residue. In this mode of existence, time feels thin, rushed, forgettable.

As Mabel Collins reminds us on *Light on the Path*, "Each man is his own absolute lawgiver, the dispenser of glory or gloom to himself; the decreer of his life, his reward, his punishment."

This emphasizes that we are the architects of our own experiences.

But the moment you begin to *choose* your tone—before action, before reaction, before words—you change the architecture of time itself.

Living deliberately means becoming a *time artist.* It means treating each human interaction, each breath, each task as a brushstroke across the canvas of your life. You bring your full self to the moment, and in doing so, the moment opens. Time stretches. Depth emerges. Meaning reveals itself.

Every conscious act becomes a sculpting of time.
When you sit down to eat, you bring gratitude.
When you walk into a room, you bring presence.
When you speak, you shape with care.

Breath, sound, silence, intention, heart focus—these are not just spiritual exercises. They are time technologies. Each one tunes your field so that the next frame collapses cleanly. They pull you out of reactive fragmentation and return you to conscious authorship.

This is the difference between living *through* time and living *with* it. In reactive mode time feels like something done to you. It drags or rushes or slips away. But when you enter coherence, time becomes responsive. It mirrors your tone. You are no longer being pulled—you are participating.

The truth is, you are shaping time whether you realize it or not. Your field is always broadcasting. Your tone is *always* collapsing the next frame. The only question is whether you're doing it by *drift* or by *design*.

Living deliberately is the invitation to stop drifting.

It is the decision to show up—to this moment, this breath, this conversation—as if it matters. Because in the architecture of consciousness, *it does*. Every coherent moment you create becomes a stabilizing node in the field. It echoes forward. It pulls future frames into alignment. It reshapes not just your personal experience but the collective timeline we all walk within. As explored in chapter 5, this is how karmic momentum is built. Every moment carries a tone. Every tone sets something in motion. And over time those tones accumulate, becoming your rhythm, your resonance, your reality.

And it begins in the smallest places.

A slow breath before you reply.
A kind word in place of criticism.
A pause before you consume another dose of noise.

These are not small acts. They are reclaims. They are the daily revolutions through which your awareness steps off the treadmill of reactivity and begins to live in rhythm with the CORE.

Thoreau withdrew into the woods to learn what life had to teach. But you don't need a forest to live deliberately. You need only to remember that this moment is not a passive flicker in time—it is an intersection of choice and vibration. You are not just experiencing it. You are shaping it.

And when you do so with awareness—again and again—eternity begins to unfold, one deliberate frame at a time.

CLOSING REFLECTION: YOU ARE THE HORIZON

This is the central realization CR has been guiding you toward—time is not an external river carrying you helplessly forward. It is a field of possibility responding to the signal you send. Your life is not unfolding *at you*. It is unfolding *from you*.

The timeline you live is the one your field stabilizes.

Everything you think, feel, and believe—each breath, each word, each emotional tone—is a broadcast. That broadcast shapes the structure of each moment. It selects which frames collapse and which remain unformed. When your tone is chaotic, your reality reflects that fragmentation. But when your tone becomes coherent—stable, harmonized, clear—the frames you collapse begin to carry the signature of that clarity. Peace arrives. Insight returns.

Synchronicity increases. The world seems to soften around you.

Eternity is a quality of *now*—a condition of consciousness where all timelines become accessible because your awareness has become still enough to perceive them. Eternity is coherence *across all tones*—the full spectrum of your being: physical, emotional, mental, and spiritual—brought into harmonic resonance with the CORE field. It is when the layers of self—physical, emotional, mental, and spiritual—come into resonance with the CORE field.

This tuning makes you potent.

You begin to see life not as a series of random events but as harmonic echoes of your own vibration. You become more deliberate with your attention, more refined in your responses. Your priorities change. Your perception deepens. The urgency of the world loses its grip on your nervous system, and you begin to hear a subtler rhythm beneath it all—the rhythm of the field responding to you.

At the edge of this realization is a kind of **sacred responsibility**.

Because if your field shapes reality, then every moment is not just a personal experience—it is a planetary contribution. You are not a spectator here. You are a horizon, a boundary between dimensions. What passes through you echoes outward. What you stabilize becomes a path others can walk.

So pause. *Breathe.* Feel the beat of your heart and the stillness behind your thoughts. The moment you choose coherence, the moment you choose love, the moment you bring awareness to the tone you carry, you step across the threshold. You become not just a person within time but a being through which time itself becomes beautiful.

And in that moment,
you are eternal.

8

THE AGE OF RESONANT HUMANITY

We all want to help one another. Human beings are like that. We want to live by each other's happiness—not by each other's misery. We don't want to hate and despise one another. In this world, there is room for everyone. And the good Earth is rich and can provide for everyone. The way of life can be free and beautiful—but we have lost the way. Greed has poisoned men's souls, has barricaded the world with hate, has goose-stepped us into misery and bloodshed. We have developed speed, but we have shut ourselves in. Machinery that gives abundance has left us in want. Our knowledge has made us cynical. Our cleverness, hard and unkind. We think too much and feel too little. More than machinery, we need humanity. More than cleverness, we need kindness and gentleness. Without these qualities, life will be violent and all will be lost.

You, the people, have the power-the power to cre-
ate machines. The power to create happiness!
You, the people, have the power to make this life free and
beautiful—to make this life a wonderful adventure.
—CHARLIE CHAPLIN, *THE GREAT DICTATOR*, 1940

THE POWER OF VIBRATION AT SCALE

The journey of CR has taken us deep into the mechanics of individual transformation. We've explored how coherence—when cultivated through breath, silence, intention, and love—can align your field, stabilize your awareness, and give rise to a new experience of time. But a deeper question now arises: What happens when this coherence is not isolated within a single life but begins to scale across the collective?

The field does not stop at the edge of the self. Your frequency does not end at your skin. Every coherent tone you carry becomes a contributor to the wider resonance of the human grid.

Just as one tuning fork can set another vibrating across a room, one coherent person—radiating clarity, integrity, and love—can entrain others without a word.

But what happens when millions begin to tune?

This is the threshold before us now, not just personal evolution but planetary entrainment.

The modern world is often described as fractured, divided, chaotic. But what if that fragmentation is not a fixed condition but an entire field out of tune? And what if the way forward is not domination but compassion?

204

Coherence is contagious. And history has shown—through spontaneous peace movements, healing circles, and the ripple effects of even a single moral voice—that the field responds when enough people stabilize a common tone.

This idea is not new. It echoes through spiritual traditions and scientific hypotheses alike. It lives in the words of visionaries such as Charlie Chaplin, who, in his final speech from *The Great Dictator*, offered not just a plea but a prophecy:

"You, the people, have the power . . . the power to create happiness! You, the people, have the power to make this life free and beautiful, to make this life a wonderful adventure."

Happiness is not meant to be a personal luxury—it is meant to be a collective vibration. And the power to create it lies not in institutions or ideologies but in the frequency of the field. When enough people begin to collapse reality from a tone of coherence, compassion, and presence, the world itself begins to reorganize.

Imagine a planet where meditation is not a luxury but a civic habit. Where education includes training in awareness and breath. Where governments optimize for citizen happiness (such as Bhutan), but coherence metrics. Where technology is designed to elevate, not isolate.

This is not utopia. It is entrainment at scale. It is what happens when vibration becomes the organizing principle of a species.

The path to this future does not require mass conversion. It requires critical mass resonance. A tipping point in tone. A network of individuals who remember their power. And who choose, again and again, to collapse frames that carry love.

Because in the end, the world we live in is not built only by action. It is built by tone.

And when enough people harmonize, Earth begins to sing a different song.

TESLA, RESONANCE, AND THE FORGOTTEN FUTURE

Nikola Tesla envisioned a world not powered by combustion, wires, or scarcity but by the resonant harmonics of Earth itself. His work on wireless electricity was demonstrable. At his Wardenclyffe Tower on Long Island—a structure that mirrored the proportions of the Great Pyramid and was intentionally built over natural aquifers—Tesla sought to transmit energy through the ground and air, tapping into Earth's own electromagnetic field. He saw the planet as a conductor and humanity as both receiver and transmitter. In his view we did not need to scar Earth to extract power—we only needed to tune to it.

And he didn't just dream it—*he did it.*

In Colorado Springs, Tesla famously lit two hundred lamps over twenty-five miles away **without wires**. Using tuned resonant coils and Earth's natural conductivity, he proved that power could be transmitted wirelessly through the air and ground. His experiments generated artificial lightning bolts over one hundred feet long and created measurable resonance in the local atmosphere. What he tapped into was the harmonics of nature itself. Tesla had, in effect, created a localized field of coherence strong enough to transmit energy invisibly.

But his vision of free energy met resistance. His most ambitious project, the Wardenclyffe Tower, was initially funded by financier J. P. Morgan. When Morgan discovered that the system would provide wireless electricity to all—without a way to meter or monetize it—he withdrew funding, stating, "If anyone can draw on the power, where do we put the meter?"

Tesla's breakthrough wasn't just technological. It was vibrational. And that may be why it was silenced.

Imagine a world without cables or wires.

Where electric vehicles, airplanes, and high-speed trains charge continuously, not by plugging in but by resonating with Earth itself. A world where energy flows invisibly through the ground and air. Where machines are not powered by extraction but by **tuning**, drawing from the natural frequency of the planet like instruments in a global symphony.

No batteries. No stations. No scarcity.
Just movement in harmony with the field.
This was Tesla's vision.

Tesla proved that energy could be transmitted invisibly through resonance. CR extends that principle into consciousness. A coherent human being, like a tuned coil, can broadcast a field that affects their surroundings—emotionally, relationally, and even biologically. As explored in chapter 2, consciousness is not confined to the brain. Minds in deep emotional or vibrational connection can become entangled systems, subtly influencing each other across space, like particles that mirror one another without contact.

In this light **a highly coherent person becomes a transmitter**.

Just as Tesla's tower could light a bulb miles away, a tuned awareness can stabilize a room, soften tension, or catalyze clarity in others— without a word. In both physics and CR, **the field does the work**. And the more coherent the source, the farther the signal travels.

Tesla's vision extended far beyond electricity. He believed vibration was the key to communication, healing, and global coherence. He spoke of frequencies that could eliminate disease. Of oscillators that could cause earthquakes if misused by governments. Of entire systems of thought, movement, and connection grounded in resonance. His notebooks contain hints at technologies lost or buried. Machines that mirrored the vibrational laws of the body, the mind, and the cosmos. His work has been suppressed for profit.

In many ways Tesla was not just inventing devices. He was prototyping a future. A civilization organized not around domination, extraction, and noise but around harmony. Alignment.

Tone.

Earth itself pulses with a natural frequency known as the **Schumann resonance**, averaging around **7.83 Hz**.

Remarkably, this matches the **alpha-theta border** of human brain waves—a range linked to **meditative states, deep relaxation, and creative flow**. Some researchers have suggested that the human brain is evolutionarily "tuned" to this Earth-based frequency and that this resonance may play a role in our emotional and mental equilibrium.

Even more striking, studies have found that **solar storms and geomagnetic disturbances** can correlate with increases in **anxiety, irritability, insomnia, and even cardiac events**. These disruptions don't just affect satellites—they ripple into our biology, potentially disrupting our natural coherence. In CR these phenomena are not seen as external forces but as reminders that **our consciousness is woven into the magnetic field of the planet itself**.

What if the reason Tesla was so misunderstood is that he wasn't speaking solely to the engineers of his day but to the people of tomorrow? To *you*?

In CR we recognize that Tesla's principles were not confined to machines. They were templates. And though his inventions may have been dismantled or suppressed, the architecture he saw is still here, hidden in plain sight. Earth still hums. The human body still emits frequencies. The field still responds to tone. What's missing is not the power source. What's missing is the coherence to access it.

Like in chapter 1 with Einstein's relativity, this is where CR picks up what Tesla began.

Because in CR we are not waiting for machines to do what only consciousness can do. We are not looking for a future built solely by external structures. We are learning to become those structures. To organize our thoughts, our breath, our relationships, and our lives around the same vibrational truths Tesla tried to map with coils and towers.

Tesla believed the universe was a system of music. CR believes the human being is the instrument through which that music becomes form.

We are the generator.
We are the tuner.
We are the civilization waiting to be resonantly born.

The future Tesla glimpsed is not lost—it is latent. We are meant to build the tone. A tone stable enough to conduct love. A tone clean enough to collapse coherent frames. A tone strong enough to remember what the ancients, the mystics, and the scientists have always known:
    That vibration is not just how the universe moves.
    It is how the universe speaks.
    And we are finally learning to listen.

THE CR FRAMEWORK FOR PLANETARY COHERENCE

CR has never been just a personal philosophy. It is a planetary operating model. What begins in the breath, in the body, and in the quiet coherence of an individual field scales. It scales through resonance. Through entrainment. Through entanglement. Through the CORE field—the invisible architecture that binds consciousness together.

The world we see around us is not simply the product of politics, technology, or economics. It is the reflection of collective tone. It is the field, broadcast and stabilized by billions of vibrational emitters—human beings. And just as one coherent person can stabilize a room, a global shift in awareness has the potential to stabilize reality itself.

In this view CR introduces not just a path to personal transformation but a structure for planetary coherence. The same practices that bring peace to an individual—breath, intention, silence, love—can, when shared and amplified, bring harmony to entire populations. When enough individuals begin to resonate with the same frequency—whether it be love, peace, or truth—a new morphic structure begins to form.

This is not hypothetical. Already, we see glimpses of this emerging structure in initiatives such as the Global Coherence Initiative by HeartMath, the communal frequency-based designs of EcoVillages, and the national policies of Bhutan, where Gross National Happiness is measured as seriously as GDP. These early models reveal a truth CR affirms: When coherence is woven into collective decision-making, the field itself becomes more livable.

Rupert Sheldrake's theory of morphic resonance helps illuminate this. He proposed that nature contains fields of memory—structures that evolve as patterns are repeated. Once a behavior, form, or frequency is stabilized, it becomes easier for others to replicate, not through transmission of information but through resonance with a shared field.

CR extends this principle to human consciousness. Every act of coherence adds weight to the field. Every time you breathe with awareness, speak with integrity, or tune yourself to love, you are not just helping yourself. You are forging a pattern that makes it easier for others to replicate. You are helping the planet remember. You are strengthening the signal of what's possible. And when enough people begin broadcasting that same signal, the field begins to tip.

Fields respond to dominant frequencies. When coherence reaches critical mass, the incoherent patterns begin to destabilize. The timelines once held in place by fear, fragmentation, and survival begin to dissolve. In their place new timelines emerge—ones shaped by clarity, compassion, and creativity.

This is how transformation unfolds. Not by force but by frequency. We do not need everyone to awaken at once. We need a stabilizing mass of coherent beings broadcasting a strong enough signal to entrain the rest. The stronger the field, the more quickly it organizes the surrounding structure.

In this sense you are not just an individual on a spiritual journey. You are a node in a planetary grid. You are a tuning fork for humanity. A beacon of light. And when you live with coherence, you don't just raise your frequency—you raise the frequency of the whole.

HEART RESONANCE AND THE SCIENCE OF ENTRAINMENT

As we explored in earlier chapters, the heart is not just an organ of feeling—it is a vibrational conductor. It emits the body's most powerful electromagnetic field, carrying not just electrical signals but emotional tone. This field can influence others even several feet away. But in the CR framework, this influence goes far beyond proximity.

When the heart enters a state of coherence—usually through feelings such as love, gratitude, or reverence—it begins to stabilize the rest of the system.

But what's more profound is that it can stabilize the people around you. The emotional signature of your field becomes an organizing force in the shared space. This is the essence of entrainment.

Earlier, we illustrated this with examples such as pendulums synchronizing on a wall or clocks aligning through shared vibration. But in collective human experience, entrainment plays out in far more dynamic ways. Consider an orchestra tuning before a performance. Each instrument begins in discord, but when one strong, steady tone is sounded, the others begin to match it. Not because they are forced to but because the field invites them into harmony. The same principle applies to consciousness.

In emotionally charged environments—a vigil, a protest, a sacred ceremony—there is often a palpable shift when coherence emerges. It's not just a mood. It's a frequency field. People begin breathing more slowly, speaking more softly, or even weeping in unison without speaking a word. These are spontaneous examples of vibrational synchrony.

Studies using heart rate monitors and EEG scans have shown that people in group meditation or synchronized breathing exercises can experience measurable alignment in both heart rhythms and brain waves—even when seated apart.[1]

Their bodies begin to entrain.

In one study pairs of people who simply gazed into each other's eyes without speaking showed synchronized alpha and theta waves after just a few minutes.[2]

When one nervous system becomes coherent, it creates a stable field that others can attune to. And once that shared frequency emerges, the group becomes something more than individuals.

It becomes a resonant system.

CR extends this by proposing that when a critical mass of people holds the same frequency—anchored in coherent emotion and awareness—they do more than affect each other. They begin to influence the timeline itself. Shared resonance doesn't just create emotional unity—it begins to collapse a shared reality. The moment itself takes on structure from the frequency they carry.

This is why emotional contagion isn't just a metaphor. It's a mechanical principle of field dynamics. One person in a high state of coherence can shift a room. But one thousand in resonance can begin shifting the culture. Over time entire narratives, institutions, and historical epochs can emerge from these coherent clusters. Not because someone imposed them but because enough people felt them into being.

You don't need to lead a movement to participate in this. You only need to understand that the tone you carry is never private. Every time you choose coherence—especially in moments of fear, reaction, or division—you are contributing a signal of alignment into the collective grid. You just need to attune yourself.

And when that signal is replicated across minds and hearts, not in uniformity but in shared harmony, the world itself begins to recalibrate.

NARRATIVE CONTROL AND COLLECTIVE TUNING

In a world saturated with information, most people believe they are forming independent opinions. What often appears to be free thinking is actually vibrational entrainment. Media, entertainment, and group ideologies are not just carriers of content—they are tuning forks for the collective field. They emit emotional frequencies that entrain the viewer's nervous system, shape perception, and steer behavior—often without conscious awareness.

This is emotional contagion at scale. A single news headline can ripple through millions of minds, triggering fear or outrage. A political slogan repeated often enough begins to resonate in the nervous system, not because it is logically true but because it has achieved emotional coherence within a group. A viral video elicits tears, laughter, or moral conviction, transmitting not just an idea but a frequency.

Recent studies in neuroscience confirm how rapidly we entrain to emotional content.[3] Outrage cycles on social media trigger dopamine releases that reinforce addictive engagement, not because the content is true but because it's neurologically stimulating.[4] This is not neutral—it is vibrational sabotage masquerading as information.

These narratives and content act like broadcast tones. They collapse frames for entire populations. They create the shared reality in which laws are made, wars are justified, and values are encoded. And while some of these narratives uplift, many are distorted. They are built to hijack attention, bypass critical thought, and manipulate resonance. Over time this can fragment the field—dividing communities, exhausting the psyche, and disorienting the individual's internal compass. *Trapping us in lower states of awareness such as fear and anxiety.*

What makes this dangerous is that it feels so personal. People think they are "waking up" when, in fact, they are tuning into negativity. They think they are resisting manipulation while unknowingly broadcasting the very frequency they absorbed. In this way the field doesn't just shape what we believe—it shapes who we become, as well as our perception and reality.

But CR offers an antidote: frequency sovereignty. The practice of tuning your own field—deliberately, daily, and with devotion—creates a kind of vibrational immunity. When you are grounded in coherence, you don't absorb every signal that passes through the collective field. You observe without being overtaken. You feel without being flooded. You also learn to filter out content that doesn't serve you. *You maintain the integrity of your signal even when the cultural environment is fragmented.*

This is what Emerson meant in *Self Reliance* when he wrote,

> *What I must do is all that concerns me, not what the people think. This rule, equally arduous in actual and in intellectual life, may serve for the whole distinction between greatness and meanness. It is the harder because you will always find those who think they know what is your duty better than you know it. It is easy in the world to live after the world's opinion; it is easy in solitude to live after our own; but the great man is he who in the midst of the crowd keeps with perfect sweetness the independence of solitude.*

This doesn't mean disconnecting from the world. It means engaging from within your own tone. You can read the news without becoming its emotion. You can listen to another's pain without collapsing into it. You can walk through a polarized world while broadcasting a frequency of peace, clarity, and depth.

In a time of narrative overload, frequency sovereignty becomes a revolutionary act. **It means you are no longer a node in someone else's story—you are a sovereign field shaping your own.** And when enough people reclaim this sovereignty, the collective narrative begins to shift. The signal strengthens. The timeline stabilizes.

And reality, once again, becomes a reflection of truth rather than manipulation.

You cannot always change the signals around you.
But you can become the signal that changes the field.

MASS INTENTION AND THE COLLAPSE OF HISTORY

What happens when large groups of people hold the same intention at the same time? In CR we understand intention not merely as thought but as vibrational command. And when that command is amplified across thousands—or millions—of coherent fields, it begins to shape history itself.

What many people don't know is that this is not speculative. It is *measurable.*

In the 1990s and early 2000s, research from the **Transcendental Meditation** movement showed remarkable results: When trained meditators gathered in groups to practice coherence together, local crime rates, violence, and even emergency room visits dropped—sometimes by statistically improbable margins. These effects occurred not because of policy changes or external interventions but because the collective field had shifted. A harmonic tone had been introduced into the local environment, and reality began to repattern itself accordingly.[5]

Supporting this, the **Global Consciousness Project** at Princeton University ran an experiment with random number generators placed around the world. These machines, which normally produce completely random sequences, began showing statistically significant deviations during moments of intense global focus, such as major disasters, New Year's celebrations, or the death of public figures. In short, when collective attention synchronized, physical systems responded. The randomness bent toward coherence.[6]

CR interprets this as more than correlation. It is evidence that shared resonance can collapse frames. When enough people hold a coherent tone—whether it is love, grief, awe, or intention—the field itself shifts. Timelines converge. New outcomes emerge. The probabilities of the moment reorganize themselves to reflect the dominant signal.

Additional studies reinforce this principle of field-based influence. In 2007 a peer-reviewed study published in *Social Indicators Research* examined large-scale group meditation events across multiple US cities and found consistent reductions in violent crime and fatal accidents correlated with periods of high coherence among meditators. These effects appeared without any physical interaction with the broader population, only the resonance of their collective field.[7]

What's more, researchers and consciousness theorists have suggested that **only a small percentage of a population**—as little as **the square root of 1 percent of a given population**—may be sufficient to create a measurable shift in the collective. For a city of 1 million people, this would require just **316 individuals** holding coherence to begin tilting the field. Like tuning forks, once a critical threshold of alignment is reached, the surrounding system begins to entrain.[8]

This is what we mean by the *collapse of history*. The future is not fixed—it is fluid. And mass intention, when harmonized through coherence, can accelerate the emergence of alternate timelines. These are not distant worlds—they are potentials already embedded in the field, waiting for resonance strong enough to stabilize them.

A visual metaphor may help: Imagine a **timeline convergence and divergence diagram**—branching pathways of human future fanning outward from the present moment. Each branch is a possibility. Most flicker in and out of phase. But when a critical mass of coherence gathers around a particular tone—say peace, compassion, or innovation—one branch strengthens. It becomes the dominant pathway. Reality "chooses" it not because of ideology but because of resonance.

EXHIBIT 8A

Timeline Convergence & Divergence

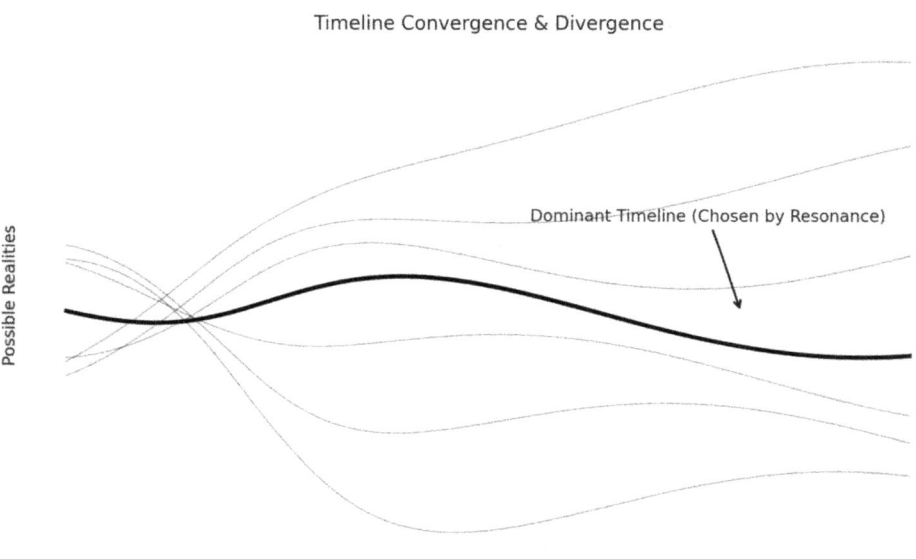

Dominant Timeline (Chosen by Resonance)

Possible Realities

Present to Future →

*Above: Each line represents a possible future branching from the present moment. The bold central path symbolizes the **dominant timeline**, stabilized by collective resonance—when enough people align with a shared tone (peace, innovation, compassion, etc.), that timeline strengthens and becomes reality.*

Every intention, every meditation, every heart-centered practice becomes a data point in the collective waveform. And when these signals align, they form standing waves of coherence—real, measurable patterns that guide the evolution of society, thought, and even planetary events.

In this way history is not something we observe. It is something we generate.

And when we gather, not in protest or panic but in stillness and resonance, we don't just hope for a better world. We collapse it into form.

THE COHERENCE GRID

Imagine a world where millions of human beings, not isolated but interconnected through the CORE field, each carry a tuned, coherent field. These fields are not passive. They are not merely personal. They are stabilizers. Signal amplifiers. Nodes in a planetary lattice of consciousness.

This is the vision of the **collective coherence grid**.

In CR we do not view coherence as a solitary achievement. We view it as the seed of a global network. Every individual who aligns with the CORE—through breath, stillness, intention, and love—becomes a point of resonance. That resonance doesn't stop at the skin. It radiates. It entrains. And it connects.

The coherence grid is a model of shared vibration. Each human field, when tuned, contributes to the stabilization of the collective. When grouped by location, affinity, intention, or spiritual practice, these fields begin to synchronize. Families, neighborhoods, cities, and nations can start to operate as regions of organized resonance, emitting clean, strong signals into the planetary field.

This is not theoretical. It is vibrational architecture. In the same way radio towers broadcast frequency, coherent humans become beacons. When many such beacons synchronize, they create a standing wave—a grid that extends beyond physical space into the structure of consciousness itself.

And this grid is intelligent.

It responds to tone, not titles. It cares not about ideology but about signal integrity. People from different cultures, religions, and traditions can all plug into it, not by thinking the same but by resonating with the same core frequency: love, compassion, coherence, and integrity.

In CR, to elevate your field is to enter the grid. You don't need to be famous or perfect. You only need to be tuned. Every act of presence, forgiveness, breathwork, or heart alignment contributes a stabilizing node. You begin to ripple stillness outward. You help anchor reality.

And the more nodes that align, the more the grid becomes self-reinforcing. Like crystals forming from solution, or iron filings aligning around a magnetic field, the collective begins to take shape around a deeper order. As we explored in chapter 3, this is the principle behind **cymatics**, where vibration sculpts matter into geometric precision. A chaotic surface becomes structured the moment a coherent tone is introduced. Events organize more harmoniously. Social systems recalibrate.

And in that hum is the future of a resonant humanity—each person not only awakening but joining a symphony. Each signal contributing to a song. Each moment of love strengthening the grid through which a new world may emerge.

MAYA, MATTER, AND THE ILLUSION OF SEPARATION

For thousands of years, ancient spiritual traditions have spoken of **Maya**—a Sanskrit word often translated as "illusion"—the veil, the dreamlike nature of the world. But Maya was never meant to imply that the world is fake. Rather, it means that what we experience is **a filtered version of reality**—shaped by our senses, our conditioning, and the limitations of our awareness. Skewed. A partial rendering of a deeper truth. In CR we reinterpret Maya not as unreality but as **misunderstood reality**—a vibrational distortion that arises when perception is out of alignment with the CORE.

What you see, touch, and believe to be "real" is not false—it is filtered through your frequency. And frequency is not passive. It is participatory. The timeline you walk, the objects you engage, the people you meet—all are collapsed through the tone you carry. Maya is not just about illusion—it is about *incoherence*.

Modern science, ironically, has begun to validate this ancient intuition. Astrophysicists now estimate that **95% of the known universe** is made up of **dark matter** and **dark energy**—substances we cannot see, cannot touch, and barely understand.[9] What we call the material world makes up only about 5% of reality.[10] So all our understanding is based on 5% of all the information available.

What appears solid is not solid. What appears still is seething with invisible forces. And what we experience as space, time, and form is but the tip of a much vaster energetic iceberg.

In CR this vast invisible layer is not empty—it is the CORE field. And Maya is what happens when we live *without* tuning to it. The illusion is not that the world isn't real but that it is **only** material and that it operates independently of consciousness.

Time and space, too, are not fixed structures. They are **reactive frequencies**, constantly reorganizing in response to your awareness. As explored in chapter 1, Einstein showed that time bends with motion, but in CR we go further: Time bends with coherence. The higher your awareness, the slower time feels because you're deepening your experience within each moment. And as shown in chapter 2, quantum experiments like the double slit reveal that observation shapes outcome—and entanglement shows that distance doesn't limit connection. The universe responds to your attention.

The more coherent your field, the clearer your perception. And the clearer your perception, the *thinner the veil of Maya becomes.* You begin to see how your thoughts shape outcomes, how your tone bends time, and how your breath changes the field.

You begin to see that the external world is not only "out there"—it is *also within you.*

This is why the core work of CR is not about denying reality but about *refining your relationship to it.*

True reality, in CR, is not what your senses detect. It is **vibrational alignment with the CORE.**

When you are tuned, life feels real in a new way, not because it becomes more fixed but because it becomes more fluid. You begin to live from inside the fabric, not outside it. You become a weaver of timelines, a sculptor of experience, **not because you "master the illusion" but because the illusion no longer masters you.**

Maya is not a prison. It is a mirror.
    And when your frequency becomes coherent, that mirror begins to reflect the divine.

ETHICS, DIVINITY, AND THE FORGOTTEN ROLE OF RELIGION

In an age of technological mastery and spiritual confusion, we have not just drifted from tradition—we have drifted from tone. We have mistaken religion for rigidity, morality for control, and devotion for dogma. But at its core, the purpose of religion was never to enforce conformity. It was to **tune the soul to coherence**. To align the human field with the divine frequency at the center of all things.

Every great spiritual tradition—before it fractured under power or politics—was an attempt to articulate resonance with God. Whether through prayer, chant, silence, scripture, or service, these practices were not merely cultural habits. They were **vibrational guidance**. Methods to stabilize the field, purify the signal, and collapse frames that mirrored the divine.

Ethics is **vibrational responsibility**. Every action you take, every word you speak carries frequency. And that frequency becomes architecture, shaping not only your own timeline but also the shared space we all inhabit. It is about maintaining coherence within the field.

When your choices are in alignment with love, truth, and humility, your signal stabilizes. You collapse cleaner frames. You ripple peace. But when your choices are made from fear, pride, or dissonance, the field reacts. You introduce chaos, confusion, and distortion, not as punishment but as natural consequence.

Religion, when stripped to its essence, was always a framework for coherence through devotion. The rituals were meant to reattune. The commandments were guardrails for vibrational integrity. The sacraments were reminders that you are not separate from the Source. Perhaps the fear of sin was about *not* making choices that would tune yourself out of harmony with the whole.

But in the modern age, we lost the map. We threw out the sacred with the superstitious. And in doing so, we inherited a world of rising noise. A planet spinning with progress but without meaning or deeper purpose, untethered to the CORE. The loss of God did not bring liberation. It brought fragmentation. Depression. Meaninglessness. A world where we can simulate anything except inner peace.

CR invites you to reclaim the wisdom buried beneath centuries of distortion. To recognize that spiritual discipline was never about control—it was about coherence.

This is why reverence matters. When you kneel, you stabilize. When you pray, you broadcast. When you align your actions with your soul's integrity, you don't just become "good"—you become whole.

And from that wholeness, your field begins to change the world.

ZERO-POINT ENERGY AND THE ENERGY OF THE SOUL

At the deepest level of physical reality, beyond atoms, beyond protons and quarks, there is not stillness but tremble. What scientists call the **zero-point field** is not a void but a fullness. It is the quantum foam from which all particles emerge. A seething ocean of latent energy, humming beneath even the coldest, most inert conditions.

According to quantum theory, even in a vacuum, where all matter and measurable energy has been removed, there remains a background field of vibration. This is not speculative. It is physics. Nobel Prize–winning physicist Richard Feynman once said, "There is enough energy in a single cubic meter of empty space to boil all the oceans of the world."

That is the power that surrounds us. That is the power that underlies everything we see.

But what if this field isn't just around us? What if it's **within us**?

Tesla may have glimpsed it first through coils and towers, but what he touched externally, we now feel internally. The zero-point field, once the domain of theoretical physics, is also the breath beneath prayer, the hum behind presence, the vast silence where miracles begin.

In CR we recognize that the zero-point field is not simply a scientific curiosity. It is the **energetic substrate of consciousness itself**. When you become coherent—when your breath, mind, and heart align into a single harmonic tone—you begin to resonate with this underlying field. You stop fighting the current. You merge with it. And in that merge, you don't *control* infinite power and knowledge—you **attune to it**. You become a receiver. A conduit. Aligned with the source.

This access is not explosive or dramatic. It's subtle. It's the deep well of energy felt in states of stillness. It's the alert calm of meditation. It's the spontaneous healing reported in moments of surrender. It's the electric inspiration that floods the artist, the monk, the mystic.

In each case the mechanism is the same: **Coherence activates access**.

The modern world has not lost its power. It has lost its **tuning instructions**. We think magic disappeared. That the age of miracles is over. But it's not. It's simply buried beneath incoherence. Buried beneath noise, haste, ego, and disconnection from Source.

When ancient yogis spoke of prana, when mystics described divine light, when saints glowed with presence, it wasn't metaphor. It was resonance. It was entrainment with the same zero-point substrate our physicists are only now beginning to measure. The soul doesn't generate its energy—it **tunes** to it.

And herein lies the future of human potential.

Our stories of superheroes—those who fly, heal, transcend time or matter—are not mere fantasies. They are **metaphors**. Cultural memory traces. Symbols of the vibrational potential of a fully tuned human being. They point toward a future not built on AI or implants but on **inner resonance**. On field mastery. On the restoration of our natural, divine design.

When coherence becomes common, so, too, will genius, healing, empathy, and extraordinary capacities that today seem rare. These are not gifts for the chosen few.

They are our birthrights.

THE UNIVERSAL RETURN: THE SELF REUNITED WITH GOD

> *In this state man comprehends his Self as a fragment of the Universal Holy Spirit. . . . This unification of the Self with God . . . is the Ultimate Object of all created beings.*
> —SWAMI SRI YUKETSWAR, *THE HOLY SCIENCE*

These words, ancient and luminous, carry the frequency of every truth CR has been guiding you toward. They are not just the closing lines of a philosophy—they are the **invitation home.**

At the heart of CR lies a simple but profound claim: The purpose of coherence is **reunion.** The realignment of the fragmented self with its eternal source. The remembrance that the consciousness pulsing through your awareness is not merely yours—it is divine in origin and destined to return.

This return is not erasure. It is fulfillment.

You are not here to dissolve into an abstract oneness. You are here to become **fully yourself** and, in doing so, realize that your self was always a tone within God's great harmony. The drop does not lose its identity when it rejoins the ocean. It **completes** it.

Coherence, then, is not a technique—it is a path of return. A tuning of your inner frequencies until they match the rhythm of the CORE field. And when that match is made, you do not lose your individuality. You become translucent to the divine. Your presence radiates something deeper than personality. It emits the tone of Source.

When all layers of the self—body, mind, emotion, and soul—come into alignment, a new level of consciousness becomes available. One where the boundary between self and God softens. You know—not believe but **know**—that your life is held, that your awareness is eternal, and that your purpose is to emit a tone of love into the world.

Because the arc of humanity is not downward. It is rising. The chaos we see in the world today is not the end—it is the **contraction before expansion**. A final fracturing before the return of resonance. Earth itself is groaning in the birth pangs of remembrance.

This is the age of resonant humanity, not as utopia but as unfolding. A time when individuals begin to awaken not just for their own peace but for the coherence of the whole. When the soul's reunion with God becomes not only a spiritual goal but also a practical frequency that reshapes time, community, and culture.

RESONANT HUMANITY BEGINS NOW

You are not just one person on a planet spinning through space.

You are a tone.

A frequency.

A signal pulsing outward into the field.

You've spent these pages not simply learning new ideas but remembering an ancient truth: that your awareness is formative. That your vibration is not a side effect of mood but the cause of worlds. And now you stand at the edge of a new understanding, not just of yourself but of humanity.

The world does not change all at once. It entrains. One tone begins to stabilize. That tone becomes a signal. That signal becomes a song. And that song spreads—quietly at first, then unmistakably—until the noise of chaos begins to organize around the rhythm of coherence.

This is how humanity transforms.
Not through conquest.
Not through algorithms.
But through resonance.

The myth of separateness is collapsing. The illusion of isolation is dissolving. You are not a single drop in the ocean. *You are the entire ocean in a single drop.* You are the bridge between the invisible and the manifest. The tuning fork through which love becomes form.

Begin with your breath. Begin with a moment of silence before a response. Begin by softening your tone, even in disagreement. Begin by remembering that the frequency you emit is not private—it is planetary. Each act of coherence is not just healing. It is history-making.

One coherent person can shift a room.
A coherent room can shift a community.
A coherent community can shift a nation.
And a coherent nation can reshape reality itself.

And it begins with you.

EPILOGUE:
THE SOURCE OF ALL COHERENCE

It is the glory of God to conceal a matter, but the
glory of kings is to search out a matter.
—Proverbs 25:2, New King James Version

This book has been a journey through awareness, frequency, and the nature of time. It has explored how reality is shaped not just by particles and physics but by perception, resonance, and intention. But beneath all that, there is something deeper still—**a Source**.

The same consciousness that collapses reality moment by moment is also the one that longs for love, harmony, and meaning. The architecture of space and time is not cold or random—it is filled with intelligent pattern, vibrational logic, and invitation.

The Creator's fingerprints are everywhere: in the structure of atoms, in the spiral of galaxies, in the frequencies of the human brain, and in the quiet whisper of the heart.

God does not hide truth to keep us away. He hides it so we'll reach for it, so we'll grow through the seeking. He conceals it the way a master artist might sign their name in the geometry of a painting so that when we discover it, we feel awe. Wonder. A sense of being known.

What you have read here is a reverent gaze at the inner workings beneath the miracle. The math of mercy. The structure of spirit. The frequency of love. And through that lens, we begin to see that our ability to shape reality is not an accident.

It's a gift.

We are *not* the source of that power.
But we are made in its image.
And so the power is entrusted to us.

And when we live in coherence—and tune ourselves to frequencies of compassion, humility, truth, and love—we begin to radiate something timeless. We don't just observe reality—we participate in its unfolding.

If your heart stirred at any point in these pages, if something ancient within you began to awaken, then this journey is just the beginning.

May you find forgiveness and compassion.
   May you walk forward more aware.
   May your resonance deepen.
   And may your life become a living echo of the intelligence and love that sustains the universe.

There is more to discover.
The mystery is holy.
And the search is sacred.

NOTES

CHAPTER 1

1. Soares, S., Atallah, B. V., & Paton, J. J. (2016). Midbrain dopamine neurons control judgment of time. *Science, 354*(6317), 1273–1277. https://doi.org/10.1126/science.aah5234
2. Sara, S. J. (2009). The locus coeruleus and noradrenergic modulation of cognition. *Nature Reviews Neuroscience, 10*(3), 211–223. https://doi.org/10.1038/nrn2573
3. Mather, M., Clewett, D., Sakaki, M., & Harley, C. W. (2016). Norepinephrine ignites local hotspots of neuronal excitation: How arousal amplifies selectivity in perception and memory. *Behavioral and Brain Sciences*, 39, e200. https://doi.org/10.1017/S0140525X15000667

CHAPTER 2

1. Rovelli, C. (2017). *Reality is not what it seems: The journey to quantum gravity*. Riverhead Books.
2. Feynman, R. P., Leighton, R. B., & Sands, M. (1965). *The Feynman lectures on physics, vol. 3*. Addison-Wesley.
3. Baggott, J. (2011). *The quantum story: A history in 40 moments*. Oxford University Press.

4. Aspect, A., Dalibard, J., & Roger, G. (1982). Experimental test of Bell's inequalities using time-varying analyzers. *Physical Review Letters, 49*(25), 1804–1807. https://doi.org/10.1103/PhysRevLett.49.1804

5. Yin, J., Cao, Y., Li, Y.-H. et al. (2017). Satellite-based entanglement distribution over 1200 kilometers. *Science, 356*(6343), 1140–1144. https://doi.org/10.1126/science.aan3211

CHAPTER 3

1. Popp, F. A., Li, K. H., & Gu, Q. (1992). *Recent advances in biophoton research and its applications.* World Scientific Publishing.

2. Blank, M., & Goodman, R. (2011). DNA is a fractal antenna in electromagnetic fields. *International Journal of Radiation Biology, 87*(4), 409–415. https://doi.org/10.3109/09553002.2010.538130

3. Montagnier, L., Aïssa, J., Ferris, S., Montagnier, J. L., & Lavallee, C. (2011). Electromagnetic signals are produced by aqueous nanostructures derived from bacterial DNA sequences. *Interdisciplinary Sciences: Computational Life Sciences, 3*(1), 81–90. https://doi.org/10.1007/s12539-011-0076-7

4. Zhou, H.-X., & Pang, X. (2018). Electrostatic interactions in protein structure, folding, binding, and condensation. *Chemical Reviews, 118*(4), 1691–1741. https://doi.org/10.1021/acs.chemrev.7b00305

5. McCraty, R., Atkinson, M., & Tomasino, D. (2009). *Science of the heart: exploring the role of the heart in human performance (vol. 2).* HeartMath Institute. Retrieved from https://www.heartmath.org/research/science-of-the-heart/

6. McCraty, R. (2003). *The energetic heart: Bioelectromagnetic communication within and between people.* HeartMath Institute. Retrieved from https://www.heartmath.org/research/science-of-the-heart/energetic-communication/

7. McCraty, R., & Childre, D. (2010). *Coherence: Bridging personal, social, and global health.* HeartMath Institute. Retrieved from

https://www.heartmath.org/research/science-of-the-heart/coherence/

8. McCraty, R., Atkinson, M., & Tomasino, D. (2001). *Science of the heart: Exploring the role of the heart in human performance (vol. 1).* HeartMath Institute. Retrieved from https://www.heartmath.org/research/science-of-the-heart/

9. Pena Ramirez, J., Fey, R. H. B., & Nijmeijer, H. (2016). The sympathy of two pendulum clocks: Beyond Huygens' observations. *Scientific Reports,* 6, 23580. https://doi.org/10.1038/srep23580

10. Goldstein, P., Weissman-Fogel, I., Dumas, G., & Shamay-Tsoory, S. G. (2018). Brain-to-brain coupling during handholding is associated with pain reduction. *Proceedings of the National Academy of Sciences, 115*(11), E2528–E2537. https://doi.org/10.1073/pnas.1703643115

11. Singh, A., & Singh, S. (2023). Study of menstrual cycle synchrony in female medical students living in a hostel. *Journal of Clinical and Diagnostic Research, 17*(1), BC01–BC04. https://doi.org/10.7860/JCDR/2023/10771221

12. Goldstein, P., Weissman-Fogel, I., Dumas, G., & Shamay-Tsoory, S. G. (2018). Brain-to-brain coupling during handholding is associated with pain reduction. *Proceedings of the National Academy of Sciences, 115*(11), E2528–E2537. https://doi.org/10.1073/pnas.1703643115

13. NTT Corporation. (2024). World's first high-definition visualization of sound waves using high-speed camera and AI. NTT Corporation. Retrieved from https://group.ntt/en/newsrelease/2024/06/17/240617c.html

14. Kröplin, B. (2005). *Welt im Tropfen: Gedächtnis und Gedankenformen im Wasser* [The world in a drop: Memory and forms of thought in water]. Stuttgart: Institute for Static and Dynamics in Aerospace Constructions, University of Stuttgart.

15. Nenonen, H. et al. (1998). Treatment of inflammatory diseases with electromagnetic fields. *Annals of the New York Academy of*

Sciences, 873(1), 356–365. https://doi.org/10.1111/j.1749-6632.1999. tb09484.x

16. Manners, P. G. (1997). Cymatics: The structure and dynamics of waves and vibrations. *Journal of Alternative and Complementary Medicine, 3*(S1), S81–S86. https://doi.org/10.1089/ acm.1997.3.s-81

17. Chaussy, C., Brendel, W., & Schmiedt, E. (1980). Extracorporeally induced destruction of kidney stones by shock waves. *The Lancet, 316*(8207), 1265–1268. https://doi. org/10.1016/S0140-6736(80)92335-1

18. Markov, M. S. (2007). Pulsed electromagnetic field therapy: History, state of the art and future. *Environmentalist, 27*, 465–475. https://doi.org/10.1007/s10669-007-9128-2

19. Crevenna, R. et al. (2012). Electromagnetic fields as cancer treatment: Early results from clinical applications. *Supportive Care in Cancer, 20*(3), 629–635. https://doi.org/10.1007/ s00520-011-1145-7

CHAPTER 4

1. Lutz, A., Greischar, L. L., Rawlings, N. B., Ricard, M., & Davidson, R. J. (2004). Long-term meditators self-induce high-amplitude gamma synchrony during mental practice. *Proceedings of the National Academy of Sciences of the United States of America, 101*(46), 16369–16373. https://doi.org/10.1073/pnas.0407401101

2. Neri, B., Callara, A. L., Vanello, N., Menicucci, D., Zaccaro, A., Piarulli, A., Laurino, M., Norbu, T., Kechok, T., Sherab, T., & Gemignani, A. (2024). Report from a Tibetan monastery: EEG neural correlates of concentrative and analytical meditation. *Frontiers in Psychology, 15*, 1348317. https://doi.org/10.3389/fpsyg. 2024.1348317

3. Lutz, A., Greischar, L. L., Rawlings, N. B., Ricard, M., & Davidson, R. J. (2004). Long-term meditators self-induce high-amplitude gamma synchrony during mental practice. *Proceedings*

of the National Academy of Sciences, 101(46), 16369–16373. https://doi.org/10.1073/pnas.0407401101

4. Flor-Henry, P., Shapiro, Y., & Sombrun, C. (2017). Brain changes during a shamanic trance: Altered modes of consciousness, hemispheric laterality, and systemic psychobiology. *Cogent Psychology, 4*(1), 1313522. https://doi.org/10.1080/23311908.2017.1313522

5. Doufesh, H., Ibrahim, F., Ismail, N. A., & Wan Ahmad, W. A. (2014). Effect of Muslim prayer (Salat) on alpha and beta EEG rhythms. *Journal of Physical Therapy Science, 26*(5), 763–766. https://doi.org/10.1589/jpts.26.763

6. Neri, B., Callara, A. L., Vanello, N., Menicucci, D., Zaccaro, A., Piarulli, A., Laurino, M., Norbu, T., Kechok, T., Sherab, T., & Gemignani, A. (2024). Report from a Tibetan monastery: EEG neural correlates of concentrative and analytical meditation. *Frontiers in Psychology,* 15, 1348317. https://doi.org/10.3389/fpsyg.2024.1348317

7. Noever, D. A., Cronise, R. J., & Relwani, R. A. (1995). Using spider-web patterns to determine toxicity. *NASA Tech Briefs, 19*(4), 82.

CHAPTER 6

1. McCraty, R., Atkinson, M., Tomasino, D., & Bradley, R. T. (2009). The coherent heart: Heart–brain interactions, psychophysiological coherence, and the emergence of system-wide order. *Integral Review, 5*(2), 10–115.

2. McCraty, R., & Childre, D. (2010). Coherence: Bridging personal, social, and global health. *Alternative Therapies in Health and Medicine, 16*(4), 10–24.

3. McCraty, R., & Zayas, M. A. (2014). Cardiac coherence, self-regulation, autonomic stability, and psychosocial well-being. *Frontiers in Psychology,* 5, 1090. https://doi.org/10.3389/fpsyg.2014.01090

4. Zaccaro, A., Piarulli, A., Laurino, M., Garbella, E., Menicucci, D., Neri, B., & Gemignani, A. (2018). How breath-control can change your life: A systematic review on psycho-physiological correlates of slow breathing. *Frontiers in Human Neuroscience*, 12, 353. https://doi.org/10.3389/fnhum.2018.00353

5. Huberman, A. D., & Spiegel, D. (2023). Brief structured respiration practices enhance mood and reduce physiological arousal. *Stanford Medicine*. https://scopeblog.stanford. edu/2023/02/09/cyclic-sighing-can-help-breathe-away-anxiety/

6. Sakaki, M., Yoo, H. J., Nga, L., Lee, T. H., Thayer, J. F., & Mather, M. (2016). Heart rate variability is associated with amygdala functional connectivity with MPFC across younger and older adults. *NeuroImage*, 139, 44–52. https://doi.org/10.1016/j. neuroimage.2016.05.076

7. Thayer, J. F., Åhs, F., Fredrikson, M., Sollers, J. J., & Wager, T. D. (2012). A meta-analysis of heart rate variability and neuroimaging studies: Implications for heart rate variability as a marker of stress and health. *Neuroscience & Biobehavioral Reviews*, *36*(2), 747–756.

8. Lutz, A., Greischar, L. L., Rawlings, N. B., Ricard, M., & Davidson, R. J. (2004). Long-term meditators self-induce high-amplitude gamma synchrony during mental practice. *Proceedings of the National Academy of Sciences*, *101*(46), 16369–16373. https:// doi.org/10.1073/pnas.0407401101

9. Lutz, A., Greischar, L. L., Rawlings, N. B., Ricard, M., & Davidson, R. J. (2004). Long-term meditators self-induce high-amplitude gamma synchrony during mental practice. *Proceedings of the National Academy of Sciences*, *101*(46), 16369–16373. https:// doi.org/10.1073/pnas.0407401101

10. Kalyani, B. G., Venkatasubramanian, G., Arasappa, R., Rao, N. P., Kalmady, S. V., Behere, R. V., & Gangadhar, B. N. (2011). Neurohemodynamic correlates of "OM" chanting: A pilot functional magnetic resonance imaging study. *International Journal of Yoga*, *4*(1), 3–6. https://doi. org/10.4103/0973-6131.78173

11. Kjellgren, A., Sundequist, U., Norlander, T., & Archer, T. (2001). Effects of flotation-REST on muscle tension pain. *Pain Research and Management, 6*(4), 181–189. https://doi.org/10.1155/2001/326893

12. van Dierendonck, D., & Nijenhuis, J. T. (2005). Flotation restricted environmental stimulation therapy (REST) as a stress-management tool: A meta-analysis. *Psychology & Health, 20*(3), 405–412. https://doi.org/10.1080/08870440412331337093

13. Feinstein, J. S., Khalsa, S. S., Yeh, H., Wohlrab, C., Simmons, W. K., Stein, M. B., & Paulus, M. P. (2018). Examining the short-term anxiolytic and antidepressant effect of Floatation-REST. *PLOS ONE, 13*(2), e0190292. https://doi.org/10.1371/journal.pone.0190292

14. McCraty, R., Atkinson, M., Tomasino, D., & Bradley, R. T. (2009). The coherent heart: Heart–brain interactions, psychophysiological coherence, and the emergence of system-wide order. *Integral Review, 5*(2), 10–115.

15. Lutz, A., Greischar, L. L., Rawlings, N. B., Ricard, M., & Davidson, R. J. (2004). Long-term meditators self-induce high-amplitude gamma synchrony during mental practice. *Proceedings of the National Academy of Sciences, 101*(46), 16369–16373. https://doi.org/10.1073/pnas.0407401101

16. Luders, E., Toga, A. W., Lepore, N., & Gaser, C. (2009). The underlying anatomical correlates of long-term meditation: Larger hippocampal and frontal volumes of gray matter. *NeuroImage, 45*(3), 672–678. https://doi.org/10.1016/j.neuroimage.2008.12.061

17. Desbordes, G., Negi, L. T., Pace, T. W. W., Wallace, B. A., Raison, C. L., & Schwartz, E. L. (2012). Effects of mindful-attention and compassion meditation training on amygdala response to emotional stimuli in an ordinary, non-meditative state. *Frontiers in Human Neuroscience, 6*, 292. https://doi.org/10.3389/fnhum.2012.00292

18. Loos, H. G. (2000). Subliminal acoustic manipulation of nervous systems. U.S. Patent No. 6,017,302. U.S. Patent and Trademark Office. https://patents.google.com/patent/US6017302A

19. Loos, H. G. (2003). Apparatus and method for manipulating the nervous system by electromagnetic fields from monitors. U.S. Patent No. 6,506,148. U.S. Patent and Trademark Office. https://patents.google.com/patent/US6506148B2

20. Tan, Z., Zhao, J., Wang, Y., Xu, H., & Zhang, J. (2023). Effects of exposure to 2650 MHz electromagnetic radiation on anxiety-like behavior in mice. *Environmental Toxicology and Pharmacology*, 100, 104044. https://doi.org/10.1016/j.etap.2023.104044

21. Zhang, J. et al. (2022). Exposure to 4.9 GHz radiofrequency electromagnetic radiation induces depression-like behavior in mice. *Environmental Research*, 214, 114078. https://doi.org/10.1016/j.envres.2022.114078

22. Liu, M., Zhang, Y., Dong, J., Sun, Y., & Zhang, J. (2023). Combined exposure to electromagnetic pulses and 4.9 GHz radiofrequency fields alters emotional behavior in mice. *Frontiers in Public Health*, 11, 1087161. https://doi.org/10.3389/fpubh.2023.1087161

23. Liu, Y., Li, H., Zhang, G., Liu, Y., Zhang, Y., & Wang, S. (2021). Effects of 1.5 GHz and 4.3 GHz microwave radiation on cognitive function and hippocampal tissue in rats. *Scientific Reports*, 11, 10168. https://doi.org/10.1038/s41598-021-89348-4

24. McCraty, R., Atkinson, M., Tomasino, D., & Bradley, R. T. (2009). *The Coherent Heart: Heart–Brain Interactions, Psychophysiological Coherence, and the Emergence of System-Wide Order*. HeartMath Institute. Retrieved from https://www.heartmath.org/research/science-of-the-heart/energetic-communication/

25. McCraty, R. (2004). *The Energetic Heart: Bioelectromagnetic Communication Within and Between People*. In P. J. Rosch & M. S. Markov (Eds.), *Clinical Applications of Bioelectromagnetic Medicine* (pp. 541–562). New York: Marcel Dekker. Retrieved from https://www.heartmath.org/research/research-library/energetics/energetic-heart-bioelectromagnetic-communication-within-and-between-people/

26. Taneja, I., Deepak, K. K., & Jaryal, A. K. (2010). Effect of slow breathing and breath holding on autonomic tone and baroreflex sensitivity in yoga practitioners. *Indian Journal of Medical Research, 152*(6), 638–647. https://pubmed.ncbi.nlm.nih.gov/34145104/

27. HeartMath Institute. (n.d.). Heart Rate Variability. *HeartMath Institute.* https://www.heartmath.org/research/science-of-the-heart/heart-rate-variability/

CHAPTER 7

1. Katahira, K., Abla, D., Masuda, S., & Okanoya, K. (2018). EEG correlates of the flow state: A combination of increased frontal theta and moderate frontocentral alpha rhythm in the mental arithmetic task. *Frontiers in Psychology,* 9, 300. https://doi.org/10.3389/fpsyg.2018.00300

2. Ulrich, M., Keller, J., & Grön, G. (2016). Neural signatures of experimentally induced flow experiences identified in a typical fMRI block design with BOLD imaging. *Social Cognitive and Affective Neuroscience, 11*(3), 496–507. https://doi.org/10.1093/scan/nsv143

3. Huskey, R., Wilcox, S., & Keene, J. R. (2022). First few seconds for flow: A comprehensive proposal of the neuropsychological mechanisms underlying flow states. *Neuroscience & Biobehavioral Reviews,* 135, 104576. https://doi.org/10.1016/j.neubiorev.2022.104576

4. Seligman, M. E. P. (2011). *Flourish: A visionary new understanding of happiness and well-being.* Free Press.

5. Csikszentmihalyi, M. (1990). *Flow: The psychology of optimal experience.* Harper & Row.

6. Gross national happiness. (n.d.). In *Wikipedia.* Retrieved from https://en.wikipedia.org/wiki/Gross_National_Happiness

CHAPTER 8

1. Paladino, S., & McCraty, R. (2020). Synchrony and coherence in collective meditation: Physiological evidence from heart rate and EEG monitoring. *Frontiers in Psychology*, 11, 540380. https://doi.org/10.3389/fpsyg.2020.540380

2. Dumas, G., Nadel, J., Soussignan, R., Martinerie, J., & Garnero, L. (2010). Inter-brain synchronization during social interaction. *PLOS ONE*, 5(8), e12166. https://doi.org/10.1371/journal.pone.0012166

3. Immordino-Yang, M. H., & Damasio, A. (2007). We feel, therefore we learn: The relevance of affective and social neuroscience to education. *Mind, Brain, and Education*, 1(1), 3–10. https://doi.org/10.1111/j.1751-228X.2007.00004.x

4. Turel, O., He, Q., Xue, G., Xiao, L., & Bechara, A. (2014). Examination of neural systems sub-serving Facebook "addiction." *Psychological Reports*, 115(3), 675–695. https://doi.org/10.2466/18.PR0.115c23z8

5. Dillbeck, M. C., Cavanaugh, K. L., & Dillbeck, S. L. (2016). Societal violence and collective consciousness: Reduction of U.S. homicide and urban violent crime rates. *SAGE Open*, 6(1). https://doi.org/10.1177/2158244016637891

6. Nelson, R. D., Bradish, G. J., Dobyns, Y. H., Dunne, B. J., & Jahn, R. G. (1998). FieldREG II: Consciousness field effects: Replications and explorations. *Journal of Scientific Exploration*, 12(3), 425–454. https://noosphere.princeton.edu/measurement.html

7. Hagelin, J. S., Rainforth, M. V., Cavanaugh, K. L. et al. (1999). Effects of group practice of the Transcendental Meditation program on preventing violent crime in Washington, D.C.: Results of the National Demonstration Project, June–July 1993. *Social Indicators Research*, 47(2), 153–201. https://doi.org/10.1023/A:1006978911496

8. Orme-Johnson, D. W., & Dillbeck, M. C. (1981). The Transcendental Meditation program and crime rate change in a sample of forty-eight cities. *Journal of Crime and Justice,* *4*(1), 25–45. https://www.researchgate.net/publication/226150037

9. Planck Collaboration. (2018). Planck 2018 results. VI. Cosmological parameters. *Astronomy & Astrophysics,* 641, A6. https://doi.org/10.1051/0004-6361/201833910

10. NASA. (n.d.). Dark Energy, dark matter. NASA Science: Astrophysics. Retrieved from https://science.nasa.gov/astrophysics/focus-areas/what-is-dark-energy

IMAGE CREDIT

Exhibit 2a

- *Image Credit: NASA/ESA/CSA/ James Webb Telescope*
- *Source: https://www.space.com/james-webb-space-telescope-detects-earliest-cosmic-web-strand?utm_source=flipboard&utm_content=other*

Exhibit 3a

- *AI-generated cymatics visualization created using OpenAI tools*

Exhibit 3b

- *AI-generated cymatics visualization created using OpenAI tools*

Exhibit 6a

- Credit: *Unknown*
- Source: https://www.surrealholistictherapy.com/single-post/the-pineal-gland-eye-of-horus
- Disclaimer: *Every reasonable effort has been made to identify the copyright holder and original source of this image. If you are the copyright holder and wish this image to be removed or credited differently, please contact us.*

ABOUT THE AUTHOR

Brandon Procak has spent over two decades exploring the relationship between consciousness, physics, and spirituality. With an MBA from Columbia Business School and experience as a CEO, board member, professor, and mentor, he has held leadership roles across frontier technologies and advised some of the world's most innovative companies, from high-growth startups to Fortune 100  giants, on how to navigate complexity and scale with purpose.

Beneath the surface of his career ran a deeper question—one that first appeared in a journal entry scribbled over 25 years ago:

"What is the relationship between time, space, and consciousness?"

That question sparked a lifetime of inquiry across disciplines—from quantum mechanics and neurology to metaphysics, ancient wisdom, philosophy, and religion.

His journey has been as personal as it is intellectual. Brandon has traveled to over 60 countries, learning from religious, spiritual, and cultural traditions around the world including time spent in the Amazon rainforest, where he participated in local ceremonies and directly encountered the vibrational shifts he now helps others understand. These immersive experiences shaped not only his worldview but deepened his core conviction: *that awareness is the architect of reality.*

www.ingramcontent.com/pod-product-compliance
Lightning Source LLC
Chambersburg PA
CBHW051612120626
46551CB00014B/1763